Because You Teach

A Dynamic Musical Resource for Innovative Staff Development

By
Kathy Hunt-Ullock, Monte Selby,
Debbie Silver, and Rick Wormeli

Incentive Publications, Inc.
Street Singer Books
Nashville, Tennessee

Illustrated by Kris Sexton
Cover by Geoffrey Brittingham
Edited by Jill Norris
Copy edited by Cathy Harber

ISBN 0-86530-227-8

1   2   3   4   5   6   7   8   9   10   09   08   07   06

PRINTED IN THE UNITED STATES OF AMERICA
www.incentivepublications.com
www.monteselby.com
www.streetsingerbooks.com

Contents

Beginning Notes

Did you ever wonder why the kid who fails to learn the twelve new vocabulary words in a chapter can listen to a new rap song and have it memorized the next day or why a slow reader who can't comprehend the main idea of a paragraph can succinctly summarize the theme of a new hit song after hearing it only once?

The answers to both questions are grounded in current brain research. Researchers report that music creates a relaxing atmosphere, establishes a positive learning state, provides multi-sensory learning experiences that improve memory, increases attention by creating short bursts of energizing excitement, and adds an element of fun to learning. So what does music research have to do with staff development? Simply put, music helps any effective facilitator or mentor to:

- Motivate teachers to remember new ideas;
- Establish a positive learning state;
- Provide multi-sensory learning experiences; and
- Energize staff development.

Because You Teach is just what you need to guarantee dynamite staff development. Four top-notch educators have created activities to model good teaching strategies and to address important staff development issues. They have matched their activities to Monte Selby's thought-provoking songs. It's an unforgettable combination.

Teachers will identify with the students personified in the engaging lyrics. The foot-tapping rhythm, rhyme, and repetition will be stuck in every listener's head and so will the important educational concepts illustrated by the activities. Choose from the large group, small group, and individual formats to encourage discussion and reinforce the teaching strategies.

Robert Sylvester, a recognized authority in brain research, observed that the arts are an exploratory enterprise that allows the brain to reconstruct the ordinary elements of life and world into something extraordinary—a celebration of the ordinary. You can turn every staff development opportunity into a celebration of good teaching with a song and thought-provoking activity from *Because You Teach*.

About the Authors

Kathy Hunt-Ullock—Kathy has been a junior high and middle school teacher, administrator, and full-time consultant/speaker. Well-known for her humor and "hands-on" approach, Kathy has presented at schools and conferences in 48 states and 14 foreign countries. She is president and founder of *Creative Solutions*, which specializes in innovative programs and practices at the middle level.

Monte Selby—Monte is an energetic advocate for educators and children. Stimulating thinking through humor, movement, interaction, and original music, his creative approach is enthusiastically received by educators, parents, and students. Monte is an experienced teacher and principal, and currently serves as an associate professor of school leadership in the Teachers College at Emporia State University. Monte is also widely recognized for his talent as a singer, songwriter, and guitarist. His music appears on network television, radio, numerous websites, school programs and videos, and is featured at national and international conferences.

Debbie Silver—Debbie is an award-winning educator with 30 years' experience as a classroom teacher and university professor. Her primary emphasis has been middle school science, but she has taught almost every grade level and every kind of student along the way. She is an internationally known consultant who has given presentations in 49 states, Canada, Asia, and Europe. Her book *Drumming to the Beat of Different Marchers* integrates research-based models, teaching strategies, management tips, and inspirational "from-the-heart" lessons for differentiating instruction.

Rick Wormeli—Rick Wormeli is an educational consultant, published author, and passionate advocate for children. A former middle school teacher with 21 years of experience, he has taught math, science, English, and history. Rick is a Nationally Board Certified teacher as well as Disney's 1996 Outstanding English Teacher of the Nation. Currently, Rick works directly with teachers and administrators around the world informing, motivating, and teaching innovative workshops and presentations. Rick has been reported in numerous media, including ABC's *Good Morning America*, *National Geographic*, *The Report of the National Commission on Teaching & America's Future*, and the *Washington Post*. Rick's book *Fair Isn't Always Equal* helps educators make sense of differentiated instruction.

Because You Teach

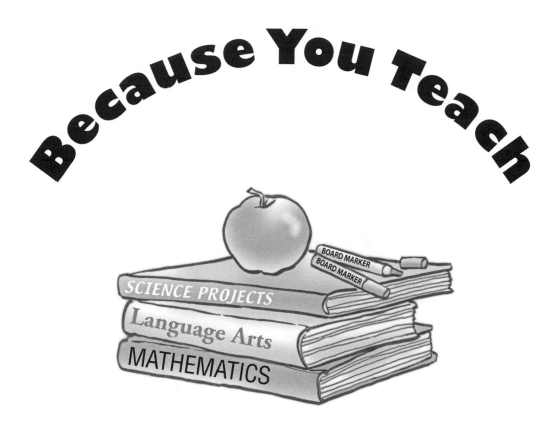

The Story Behind the Song

This is a song that is more relevant today than it was when it began over ten years ago at a teachers' retreat in Kansas. I met and sang with the teachers. I listened to what they were talking about, held onto their thoughts, and finally put them into a song just before a recording session. "Because You Teach" is all about the balance between what's new and what's important, and about the challenges of keeping up with today's kids.

–Monte

Staff Development Ideas by Rick Wormeli

The Focus

It's easy to get overwhelmed in today's teaching world. Educators must keep up with the latest in each "'ogy"—*pedagogy, technology, biology, psychology*—and every "'acy"—*literacy, bureaucracy, numeracy, diplomacy*—all while dealing with classroom management, individual student needs, apathy, meetings, paperwork, school politics, students' parents, re-certification issues, AYP, supply orders, their own physical and emotional needs, public outcry, long commutes, and the fact that someone accidentally removed an eagerly anticipated lunch from the teachers' lounge refrigerator. What's an optimist to do?

For many students, it's a world of click-on-the-Website-icon, download-the-page-in-seconds-quickly, flash-to-the-next-image, MTV, BET, fill-my-iPod-with-10,000-tunes, show-me-what-I-don't-know attitude. In order to survive, they listen and focus selectively, and their choices are not always the ones teachers would make. Many students thrive in this whirlwind and are impatient with those who ask them to slow down, explore, or contemplate. They insist on cutting to the chase, pleading for the *Spark Notes* version of what it all means and what will be on the test. They willingly give up their own autonomy and dreams, indoctrinated early on that: *when success is important, the teacher's way is the safe way.*

This kind of education will not protect democracy, of course, but the questionable emphasis on high-stakes testing makes every student's crusade a battle for the "right" answer. Many students decry experiences that make them think beyond parroting what the textbook said.

Educators have noted that today's sixth- graders already know more than a medieval man would know in the course of his entire lifetime. The question is whether or not today's students have the wisdom to process and use the knowledge compassionately, and to continue to learn without losing their individuality. Thoughtful, dedicated teachers are the critical factor.

The Song

The frenetic nature of *Because You Teach* expresses the quick pace of a teacher's struggle to keep up with students and society. It recognizes that it will take some quick pedaling to first reach, and then teach today's students. Teachers must:

- stay on top of the game with new thinking;
- question conventional practice often;
- keep up with the latest ideology in cognitive science as it applies to classroom learning; and
- rediscover the lost art of quiet reflection and pass it on to students.

The Hook

Given today's new and often harried world, are you ready to do what it takes? You are a professional educator and your mission is important. Because you dedicate yourselves to students, handle all of teaching's inherent stresses, and smile each morning, we lift you up. You're the best hope for our future—because you teach.

Because You Teach

So you're teachin' in a new age
Everything fast change
Try to give 'em what they need
Learn a high-tech technique
Try it out next week
To help the kid that doesn't read
But you're teachin' in an old class
It's too hot, a tough task
Feelin' like you can't compete
With the TV, computer tower
Calculator, solar power
How you gonna make 'em think?

You got kids on the Internet
World-wide web-head
Everything under the sun
They're talkin' on a cell phone
Call waiting, dial tone
New ways to get more done
Send a fax, grab some fast food
Hypermart, drive-thru
Program their VCR
They play with toys that can do it all
Shop at home or in the mall
And that's just the way things are

These kids don't want to memorize
They hate the mental exercise
Unless they think it can relate
Regurgitate a list of names
Famous men, heroic dames
But how does it affect their fate?
They need to know what's comin' up
What happens when they are adults
The farmer, lawyer, and the clerk
And the knowledge that they want real fast
Is in the future not the past
Competing in the world of work
But they still need to socialize

Still need to realize
Communication is the key
They need the skills to work together
Solve problems, make a better
World for the grandkids of you and me
And when you're teaching
        the whole child—
The happy, sad, the hog-wild
The hero and the sinking ship.
They learn from hard work, big dreams
Good hearts, honesty:
The value of relationships

Yeah, you're teachin' on a new page
Ridin' on a fast wave
It's tougher each and every day
There are some kids with too much stuff
Others never had enough
You try to meet their needs
In innovative new ways
But the work you do is so important
Every single school mornin'
Put the future in their reach
You deserve respect and admiration
For the work in your profession . . .

Activities for a Large Group

Stand for a Student

Purpose:

Sometimes we get overwhelmed with the busy-ness of what we do every day. On these days, we can lose sight of why we do what we do. It's during these times that we need to step back and focus on the students and moments that give our jobs meaning. This activity will help teachers to rededicate themselves to their roles as educators, to personalize their missions, and to remind them that students are more than one more paper to grade. Standing for a student publicly can re-charge us and transform the overall tone of the faculty.

Materials:

Step-by-step:

> ♪ Note: This activity can be very emotional for teachers. One or more teachers will probably well up with tears. It's amazing how close to the surface our emotions run as we work intensely all day long with students, then publicly describe a student or moment that touched us in some way.

1. Identify three or more teachers willing to *stand for a student* prior to your gathering. Give them a day or two to consider what they want to say.

2. During a faculty meeting or gathering, allow each of the identified teachers a few minutes to declare for whom they are standing. Each teacher begins with "I stand for . . ." and completes the phrase with the name of a student for whom they advocate. The identified students are usually ones <u>for whom the individual teachers have made a difference</u>. Teachers can also stand for students who:
   - require a bit more (or a lot more) attention from us
   - have turned a corner somehow after a long struggle
   - make an important and personal discovery about themselves
   - make major contributions to the school or community
   - demonstrate unusual kindness, ethics, and/or integrity
   - give us hope
   - have unusual circumstances in their lives
   - cause stress in everyone who teaches them
   - are in danger of losing hope

> ♪ Note: I would suggest you do this only a few times a year, and maybe only once a year, as it can lose its effectiveness with overuse.

Serious challenges or positive turns, small moments or dramatic leaps, the students are chosen for a variety of reasons. All of them, however, are students who make us personally rededicate our efforts.

Here's one example from middle school art teacher Eric Baylin, who shares this "I stand for . . ." response regarding one of his former students:

"I stand for Benno. Middle school students (and maybe everybody else) typically divide the world into those who are 'good' at art, and all the others. They mostly end up in the 'other' camp. Benno definitely considered himself one of the 'others.'

Earlier this year as an 8th-grader, Benno was drawing his hand from observation, a 'simple' exercise to help students look more closely at the world. His first efforts came out looking like all the hands he had drawn since lower school, a simplified idea of a hand but not a direct observation. We walked around the room looking at one another's efforts. He noticed how accomplished many of the others were and expressed his frustration at not being very good at this.

When Benno got back to his seat he started to draw again but with a new intensity in his focus. He was figuring something out: how he could trust his eyes in a new way. He started with his thumb and very excitedly called me over. 'Look at this, it actually looks like a thumb.' This was learning made visible; his excitement was palpable. He continued to draw an extremely competent image of a hand.

The difference between the first and second efforts was remarkable. Classmates came over to see his drawing and congratulated him. Their support and encouragement were as wonderful as Benno's discovery. When we switched to working on paintings later that semester, Benno discovered that he had an eye for mixing subtle gradations of colors. Suddenly painting, which had never appealed to him, became a new adventure.

I love Benno's determination and courage to grow beyond his limited expectations. Could I have stayed in the classroom for 36 years if it weren't for all the Bennos bravely opening up to new worlds within themselves?"

3. On another day, as you and the faculty feel comfortable, invite three or four more teachers to stand up and share for whom they stand.

Rocks in a Jar

Purpose:

To help teachers prioritize scarce resources of personal time and energy based on what's most important; and to help teachers distinguish what is important from what is urgent

Materials:

• A faculty gathering

> ♪ Note: Conduct a dry run of this demonstration a day or two ahead of time to make sure you have the right ratios of small, medium, and large rocks. Just as in life, experience provides the insight we need to make sure we have the right ratios of small, medium, and large importance tasks to fit into our jar (life). The impact of the metaphor dims if you do not have the correct proportions.

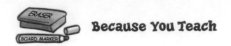

- Rocks of three different sizes: sand and pebbles, medium-sized rocks, large rocks
- A large jar such as a pickle or pretzel jar found at discount warehouse grocers
  (All of the rocks must fit into the jar.)
- Small containers to hold the rocks as you remove them from the jar

Directions:

You will fill a large jar with different-sized rocks in two different ways.

1. Explain, "As we run around in our lives, we often spend a lot of time working on the small, everyday urgencies that fill our time." (List a number of these specifically, such as returning phone calls, sharpening pencils, erasing the chalkboard, social conversations, filing materials, moving furniture, and responding to e-mail.) As you mention each example, drop bits of sand or a small pebble into the empty jar.

2. List medium-sized urgencies that rule our lives, dropping the medium-sized rocks into the jar as you say each one. (These can be tasks such as attending meetings, attending a church/synagogue/mosque/community meeting, grading homework, or buying a new couch.)

3. Finally, list the big rocks of your life. These are the most important things in your life that would dramatically and negatively transform you if they were removed. (These might include getting married, the birth of a child, living in a safe community, exercising, sleeping, eating a healthy diet, managing stress, and working on relationships with family members.) As you list these, add the largest rocks to the jar.

4. Note that the sand, pebbles, and medium-sized rocks fill the jar quickly. There is little room for all the large rocks—the most important parts of our lives—in the jar. Some of the important parts are actually left out, and the jar represents lives filled with hundreds of small urgencies, but nothing large and meaningful.

5. Now empty the jar. Then, follow the same procedure again, but this time start with the most important aspects of life as you narrate, then move to the medium-sized ones, and then list the small, everyday urgencies. Put the large rocks into the jar first. Fill the air spaces left in the jar around the large rocks with the medium-sized rocks. Finally, fill in the remaining space in the jar with the sand and small pebbles. You will find that you can fit everything into the jar (life) if you emphasize the most important parts first.

6. Once the two demonstrations are done, ask participants to consider possible connections to their own busy lives. Ask them to identify small, medium, and large *rocks* in their own lives, then how to keep sight of our professional goals and duties but not let the urgent overwhelm the important.

The activity *Rocks in a Jar* is based on an idea from Stephen R. Covey's book,
The Seven Habits of Highly Effective People.

Activities for a Small Group

Why Teach? Gallery Walk

Purpose:

To develop camaraderie among staff as they cope with the daily struggle to keep up with students and the teaching life

Materials:

- Faculty separated into small, heterogeneous groups
- Newsprint
- Colored markers for each group

Step-by-step:

Part I

1. Group teachers heterogeneously in small groups. Groups should mix grade levels, regular education, special education, core, and encore (elective/specialist) teachers.

2. Ask one person within each group to record the responses to the given questions anonymously on newsprint that can be posted for all to see.

3. Now, have group members share responses to the following questions with one another:
   - How did you get into teaching?
   - What are the positive aspects of teaching?
   - What are the frustrations in teaching?
   - What's one professional goal you have for yourself this year, and how are you going to accomplish it?

> ♪ Note: The recorder should capture the gist of each person's comments on the newsprint, but add more commentary as the group exchanges ideas. Allow 10 to 15 minutes or less for this portion of the experience.

Part II

1. Post the pages of newsprint around the room.

2. Ask groups to move to each newsprint page other than their own for a period of three to five minutes. The group is to read the comments recorded and make a response to what they read. Responses can be words of encouragement, clarifications, additional ideas/suggestions, personal reactions to what was written, respectful disagreements, and anything else that they want to say as long as the comments are professional and supportive of the writer.

Option: Post the Part I newsprint comments in a commonly visited place such as a teachers' lounge for a week. Ask faculty members to write comments on them over the course of the week.

3. Record all the comments from the posters onto a few sheets of paper (or into an Internet folder) and share them with participants. Ask teachers to comment on what they notice about the remarks—patterns, visions for the school, ideas for themselves, surprises, etc.

Activities for Individuals

Advice to Administrators

Purpose:

To help teachers identify what helps them persevere in their busy, stressful lives

Materials:

- Time for teachers to reflect individually
- A surface and medium for recording individual thoughts

Step-by-step:

1. Ask teachers to make a list of all the ways administrators could help them:

   - Positively handle the quick pace and stresses of teaching and learning

   - Find meaning and satisfaction in their jobs as teachers

   - Feel appreciated by the administration

   Sample items on the list might include:

   - Take over a teacher's classroom for one period, giving that teacher an extra period to plan or exercise.

   - Rotate faculty meeting locations among teachers' classrooms.

   - Set up Intranet folders dedicated to topics teachers want to study.

> Note: This is not to say that these three foci are the exclusive domain of the administrators. Teachers are responsible for figuring these out as well. The list has two purposes: First, to give some great advice to administrators on which they will hopefully act, and second, for teachers to explore what makes them inspired and motivated. The list is a hook on which teachers hang their own self-discoveries.

- Begin a school-wide wellness program for teachers. This includes the following areas: physical exercise, diet, stress management, global action, sleep, relationships, and weight management.
- Find money for every single teacher to attend at least one professional development conference during every school year.
- Provide enough paper for the entire school year, instead of teachers having to purchase their own.
- Start a Critical Friends, Teacher Action Research, or Professional Learning Community group within the faculty.
- Keep faculty meetings to topics that can be discussed only when the faculty is gathered, not a litany of items that can be written down and read by the faculty members.
- Provide free coffee and chilled bottled water to faculty members for an entire day.
- Provide duty-free lunch periods for all staff.
- Provide a mentor program for new teachers as well as interested veteran teachers.
- Provide business cards for all faculty members.
- Share moments of inspired teaching within the faculty with the staff.
- Help faculty members create personal professional goals that will significantly and positively impact their work in the coming year.
- Purchase individual copies of professional books for every teacher that they can keep for the duration of their career.
- Provide free daily shoulder and neck massage with scented oils—okay, this may be a stretch, but a teacher can hope.

2. Ask teachers to think quietly and reflectively about their impact on students.
   - Does their teaching matter? If so, how? If not, why not?
   - Do they have positive impact on students and the community? If so, what evidence do they have that they do? If not, why not?
   - What could they do to have more positive impact?

3. Facilitate a way for teachers to share their reflections with one other faculty member. Reflections shared carry more weight with most of us. We think about them more deeply, they stay with us longer. In addition, our listening partner's response often helps us see things our personal myopia prevents us from seeing.

Family Tree

The Story Behind the Song

Debbie Silver and I started the idea for this song based on the comment teachers sometimes say after meeting a child's parents—"no wonder Sam is the way Sam is . . ." Sarcasm can be funny, but it can be equally dangerous in education as it shapes attitudes and beliefs. This song is intended to remind us that if kids absorb unwanted characteristics of parents and other adults, they can also gain positive attributes from being around great role models. On a larger scale, if we are careful to look at negative, sarcastic statements as an opportunity to make positive change, we can create better experience for students— who will be our next set of school parents. Debbie and I hope the first verse makes you laugh. We hope the remainder of the song makes you think!

—Monte

Staff Development Ideas by Debbie Silver

The Focus

It is vital today to enlist appropriate support from parents. These activities give staff members a chance to practice effective ways to gain the respect of parents while soliciting their support.

The Song

The entertaining lyrics "those apples don't fall far from the family tree" from the song "Family Tree" are deceiving. The words are not offered as an excuse. The song is a challenge to educators to do whatever they can to battle familial negative traits. It encourages educators to help turn things around for students and their families.

The Activities

In the large group activity, faculties can have a little fun with role-playing while they focus on key words and actions that help ensure parent conferences work for the best interest of the student. Novice teachers can gain insight, tips, and well-chosen words from veterans, and all participants get a chance to reflect on the importance of the home/school connection. A second choice for the large group activity begins with a humorous skit highlighting teacher-parent communication problems. A discussion follows about word choices, educational jargon, and other factors that influence understanding between these student-advocates. In small group activities, participants explore the concepts of student-led conferences and methods for getting more parents involved. Individual activities include reflective exercises on the teacher's own conferencing skills and an opportunity to do some proactive planning for better teacher-parent communications.

Family Tree

She may look just like her mother but she acts just like her dad
The teachers all say it's genetic—family DNA is bad
While experts look hard for an answer her prescription running low
No two agree on one solution, but consensus says they know.

CHORUS:
> Those apples don't fall far from the family tree
> One generation's unique traits can pass down—eternally
> Sometimes it's for the better; sometimes it's sad to see
> Those apples don't fall far from the family tree.

It's not a hopeless case because the hopeless have a chance
To make a good change for the better till the species can advance
All those behaviors that we teach and model can become routine
Until new habits pass on down through both the mom and daddy's genes.

CHORUS:
> Those apples don't fall far from the family tree
> One generation's unique traits can pass down—eternally
> Sometimes it's for the better; sometimes it's sad to see
> Those apples don't fall far from the family tree.

Don't think I think there's only one way we should all behave and speak
I know our differences are healthy; we all have weaknesses and strengths
But, if we all look in the mirror and improve in some small way
Before too long we've changed the world into a whole lot better place
(It's up to me to make that change . . . because)

CHORUS:
> Those apples don't fall far from the family tree
> One generation's unique traits can pass down—eternally
> Sometimes it's for the better; sometimes it's sad to see
> Those apples don't fall far from the family tree.

– Monte Selby and Debbie Silver
©2004 Street Singer Music, BMI/Toto Tunes, ASCAP

Activities for a Large Group

Parent Conference Role-Play

Novice teachers in particular are sometimes intimidated by meeting individually with parents. Teachers new to your school may be unaware of some of the "hidden agendas" among the parental community. It is helpful to role-play some possible parental conference scenarios so that teachers get a chance to discuss solutions, craft their specific wording, and think about their desired outcomes of such meetings. This activity is designed to generate teacher solutions and group camaraderie.

Purpose:

- To clarify the importance of teacher-parent partnerships

- To consider specific assertive but parent-friendly approaches to conferencing

- To practice strategies and effective language for conferencing

Materials:

- Chairs and a staging area for role-playing

- Copies of the possible scenarios on pages 27 and 28

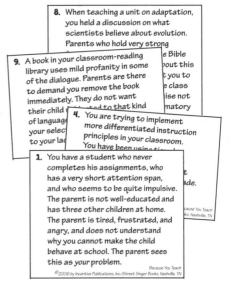

Step-by-step:

This is a role-play activity that can be entertaining, insightful, and pragmatic.

1. You may want to start by having some of your more demonstrative teachers participate in a preview for the whole group of how the activity works. Depending on the size of your staff, continue the activity as a whole group or have teachers break out into smaller groups of 8 to 10.

2. In each instance an emcee selects a scenario (at random or of their own choosing). The emcee assigns the roles of parent(s), teacher(s), and an administrator (optional). Participants are encouraged to play their roles as honestly and as accurately as they can.

3. Laughter and levity are to be expected (and encouraged), but it is important for the emcee to keep players focused on realistic suggestions and solutions.

4. The emcee sets up the scenario for the non-performers. The performers role-play the situation for 5 to 7 minutes. The emcee keeps time and calls an end to the role-play when time is up or when the issues have been addressed.

5. Non-performers write down words and phrases the performers say that they agree with as well as suggestions for changes. Non-performers cannot speak during the presentation.

6. At the end of the presentation, the emcee directs the discussion by asking:

   • Who won?
   The answer can be *everyone, no one, the teacher,* or *the student.*
   However, it is important to emphasize that the goal in every parental interaction is to promote what is best for the student. Anything that interferes with what is in the best interest of the student is a loss.

   • Was this depiction reasonable? In what ways was it realistic, and in what ways was it not?

   • Was there any justification in what the parent(s) said or did? In what ways did they "have a point"?

   • What was the body language of the participants? Is body language important? Why or why not?

   • Were all the comments and actions of the teacher(s) proactive and professional? Why or why not?

   • Do you have a suggestion about another way this could be handled? (Any "tricks of the trade" you can share?)

7. Performers are then encouraged to tell how it felt to take on the role they had. They are given the chance to say what they might do the same or do differently next time.

8. Ask teachers to clarify what kind and level of support they would like to have from their administrator(s) in parent meetings. Administrators should not contribute ideas or critiques unless specifically asked a question by the teachers (and then keep answers focused on legal issues rather than on personal opinions).

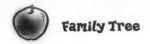
Teacher to Parent: Can You Hear Me?

Purpose:

To examine the importance of word selection

Materials:

Copies of Debbie Silver's "The Parent Conference" (page 29)

Step-by-step:

1. Before the activity, ask two volunteers to be ready to read "The Parent Conference." The volunteers should assume the parts of Teacher One and Teacher Two. Encourage the Teacher One player to be very professional, vague, and aloof. Teacher Two should be grumpy, crotchety, and hateful (in a humorous way).

2. Have the two teachers perform.

3. Discuss the poem and teachers' reactions to the two characters.

   • Which teacher was the better communicator? Why?
   Most people agree that Teacher Two is much too negative, but does Teacher One really give the parent valuable information?

   • What are some examples of "educational jargon" that sometimes is confusing or irritating to parents? Can you think of some more constructive, applicable terminology that could be used instead of phrases like "language-deficient," "hyperactive," "unmotivated," etc.? Can you name other examples?

   • What is the ultimate purpose of every teacher-parent conference? What are some things teachers can do to ensure that they always act as the student's advocate?

> ## Activities for a Small Group

Considering Student-Led Conferences

Purpose:

   • To acquaint participants with information about student-led conferences
   • To explore the advisability of having student-led conferences at the participants' school

Materials:

Copies of excerpts from NMSA's "The What, Why, and How of Student-Led Conferences" and/or copies of other articles about student-led conferences

♪ Note: If your school has not tried using student-led conferences, before beginning the activity distribute articles and information about these conferences and give teachers time to review the information.

Step-by-step:

1. Divide the group into opposing sides and ask them to debate the pros and cons of using student-led conferences at your school. Teachers need not be in agreement with the side they represent, but they should try to argue passionately for the view they are assigned.

2. Process the debate.
   - Was it won because of a particular argument?
   - Does that argument apply to your school situation?
   - Would student-led conferences be beneficial to your school community?

Getting Parents More Involved

Purpose:
- To explore reasons that parents are not more involved
- To generate additional means of enlisting parental support

Materials:
- Poster paper
- Markers

Step-by-step:

Part A

1. Have the group brainstorm ideas about why parents are not more involved in your school. On the group's poster, list any reasons you know or suspect that some parents are hesitant to come to your school.

2. On a second poster, list all of the things your school or individuals in your school are currently doing to try to get more parents involved. Beside each word on the list, write a word or phrase evaluating its effectiveness: "working," "not working," "kind of working," or "don't know yet."

3. Compare the two posters to see if there are gaps between perceived problems for parents and solutions being tried by the school.

4. On a third poster, list some possible strategies the school as a whole and individual teachers could use to help motivate parents to be more involved in their children's education.

Part B

1. Brainstorm ways parents could help the school (besides directing fundraisers). Include both large and small jobs.

2. Compile your ideas as a checklist you can send home to parents asking them to indicate the things they would be willing to do. Be sure to include specific job descriptions, including precisely what would be required, how much time it would take, and other important data. Provide a place for parents to tell you how much time they are willing to give. Have designated volunteers (parents) follow up and schedule other parents to help.

Activities for Individuals

Parent Conference Reflection

Purpose:
- To help individuals think about their own experiences in dealing with parents
- To help teachers analyze their interactions with parents

Materials:
- Journal or computer
- Pen or pencil or computer paper

Step-by-step:

1. In your journal write about at least one meeting you had with a parent that did not go as well as it could have.

2. List things you would do differently next time and tell why.

3. Consider what you learned from this experience that you will carry into your next meeting with a parent.

Teacher Outreach

Purpose:

To encourage teachers to initiate a positive contact with the parents of every child

Materials:

- Student records
- Templates and/or spreadsheet software

Step-by-step:

1. Generate a list of every student you teach. Include the parents' names, addresses, and phone numbers.

2. Set a goal for how many parents you will contact each week with a positive comment.

3. Keep a record of whom you call or write. Make notes beside each name about what you said or wrote. (Remember, this contact is to be a positive, encouraging message.)

Create a Parent Resource File

Purpose:

- To encourage teachers to begin a collection of resources to help parents better understand the problems and solutions to their particular situation

- To keep teachers current on topics regarding typical characteristics and predicaments of their student population

Materials:

- Access to NAESP's electronic newsletters, *Middle Matters* and *School & Community News Today*

- Various journals, periodicals, and other sources of information for parents

- Annotated bibliographies about books that are helpful to parents

♪ Note: Parental information sheets written in both English and Spanish are available from the National Association of Elementary School Principals—NAESP. They are provided to members in their newsletters with permission to reprint. Topics cover everything from dealing with bullies to healthy food choices to overscheduled children to fostering honesty in kids. It is a good idea to form an "exchange club" at your school so that all teachers get copies of relevant and helpful information for parents who are interested.

Step-by-step:

1. Create files of brief handouts and articles on various topics of concern to parents. Make sure they are simple, to the point, and easy to read. Include a bibliography

when appropriate. At parent conferences have your files available so that you can pull out information sheets to give to parents (for them to keep).

2. Create a book list on various topics of concern to parents. Poll other teachers for recommendations of helpful books for parents. When parents ask for help or more information, give them a copy of the list with a notation about which book(s) you think they will find beneficial.

Personal Reflections

Purpose:

- To help teachers clarify their roles as advocates for students
- To give teachers an opportunity to reflect on the importance of the home/school connection

Materials:

- Teacher journals
- Copies of the following quotes

Step-by-step:

Choose one of the following parent comments and respond to it in your journal.

- As a parent, I leave my child with you each day that you may instill in him all the concepts of life. You teach him sharing so he understands nothing is of value unless it is shared. You teach him art so the radiant colors of the world will not pass him by. You teach him letters so words may become his tool to help make this planet a gentler place. You teach him time so he comes to know nothing lasts forever, especially childhood . . . You teach him about acceptance so he learns not all of life is fair. You are my child's teacher, and there is no better thing to be.

  —Robyn Keough

- Good teachers make being a parent a little easier. Being a parent isn't always easy. It's such a big responsibility to direct another person's life— you often wonder if you're doing everything right. I imagine that teachers feel some of the same things that parents do. Though their work is to teach, they do more than that. They are counselors, role models, and often friends. They are to be thanked for all they do to make a parent's job a little easier.

  —Taylor MacKenzie

Possible Role-Play Scenarios:

1. You have a student who never completes his assignments, who has a very short attention span, and who seems to be quite impulsive. The parent is not well-educated and has three other children at home. The parent is tired, frustrated, and angry, and does not understand why you cannot make the child behave at school. The parent sees this as *your* problem.

Because You Teach
©2006 by Incentive Publications, Inc./Street Singer Books, Nashville, TN

2. One of your "A" students recently failed a major exam. Her parent is highly involved in every aspect of the daughter's life and is quite upset by this grade. The parent wants to know if you can give the student extra credit assignments to make up for the low test score. The parent informs you that you are the only teacher who has given the daughter less than an "A," and the parent wants an explanation.

Because You Teach
©2006 by Incentive Publications, Inc./Street Singer Books, Nashville, TN

3. You are a novice teacher. The parent is a veteran teacher who is well-known for being opinionated and a bit of a bully. The parent is questioning your decisions on classroom rules, consequences, and grading policies. The parent is upset with a consequence you gave the child and wants you to change your decision.

Because You Teach
©2006 by Incentive Publications, Inc./Street Singer Books, Nashville, TN

4. You are trying to implement more differentiated instruction principles in your classroom. You have been using tiered assignments and alternative assessments. An "A" student did not make his usual top grade. The parent is questioning the fairness of your grading.

Because You Teach
©2006 by Incentive Publications, Inc./Street Singer Books, Nashville, TN

5. You have noticed a marked difference in the attitude and effort of one of your female students. She has become withdrawn, sullen, and unmotivated. She no longer associates with her peer group, and she sometimes displays inappropriate anger. You have asked her what is wrong and have gotten no response. You are worried that something is wrong at home. The parent insists that nothing is wrong.

Because You Teach
©2006 by Incentive Publications, Inc./Street Singer Books, Nashville, TN

6. One of your students has very affluent parents who travel a great deal for both business and pleasure. The student is a member of a classroom team that has been working on a major project scheduled for presentation two days before Spring Break. The parents are here to inform you that they are taking their entire family on a ski vacation "a little early." They want to make sure that you *do not* penalize their child for missing school the week before Spring Break.

Because You Teach
©2006 by Incentive Publications, Inc./Street Singer Books, Nashville, TN

7. A theft has occurred in your room. A significant amount of cash was taken from a young lady's purse sometime during the day. You suspect another girl who has a history of dishonest behavior. A boy in your class reported that he saw the suspected girl stuffing several bills into the bottom of her book bag. The suspect vehemently denies that she has stolen anything and says you always suspect her for things she did not do. You've asked the parents to come for a conference. The parents are adamant that their child would never steal.

9. A book in your classroom-reading library uses mild profanity in some of the dialogue. Parents are there to demand you remove the book immediately. They do not want their child subjected to that kind of language, and they believe that your selection of this book speaks to your lack of morals.

8. When teaching a unit on adaptation, you held a discussion on what scientists believe about evolution. Parents who hold very strong fundamentalist views on the Bible are there to speak to you about this "misinformation." They want you to retract what you said to the class about evolution and to promise not to mention any such "inflammatory opinions" again.

10. You suspect that one of your students has learning disabilities. His parents contend that the only thing wrong with him is that the school has failed to motivate him. They have refused to have the child tested because they don't want him labeled as "special ed." They maintain that nothing is *wrong* with him. They tell you that if the school were doing its job, their son would be working on grade level.

11. You work in a socioeconomically diverse school. You are the sponsor of the sixth grade end-of-year celebration. A group of parents has come to talk with you about possible plans for the event. They want to make it a formal evening event. They would like to hold a dance at the local country club. Students will be required to buy or rent formal attire. The parents have a list of limo services that are willing to give a 15% discount to any families who choose to hire them to chauffeur their students to and from the dance. The parents want you to require that all students have dates and that boys be encouraged to buy corsages for the girls. This was supposed to be a meeting to discuss ideas, but it is obvious they have already decided exactly what they want to have happen. These parents are very *politically connected*.

Make up your own scenarios. Draw from your own experiences or those you have heard about at your school. Do not identify any of the players by name, even if everyone knows whom you are talking about.

Reproduce this page at 120% for 8½ x 11 size.
Use it with the activity on page 22.

The Parent Conference

Teacher One	Teacher Two
So glad that you could come today.	Where have you been all year?
There's just so much I have to say.	I've had it up to here!
His curiosity is vast.	He's nosy as can be!
His work is finished very fast.	He does it carelessly!
Your son is quite theatrical.	A show-off to the end!
And really very practical.	He's selfish and won't lend!
Imagination quite renown.	The kid is full of lies!
And quite assertive, I have found.	My orders he defies!
Reminders daily are in vain.	He cannot keep a rule!
His motivation seems to wane.	He's lazy as a mule!
You've reared him inhibition-free.	His bathroom jokes are sick!
And gross control needs work, I see.	He's clumsy as a stick!
Tactile learning is his style.	He knocks the kids all flat!
His social skills will take a while.	Your son's a spoiled brat!
He's challenging, I will confirm.	He's crazy, I believe!
I'm looking forward to next term.	I've just applied for leave!

by Debbie Silver

The Story Behind the Song

Rick Wormeli and I wrote this song together at a National Middle School Association convention. Rick shared his poem "September Plea" with me. I was struck with the thought that if all students' dreams for life were limited by their current behaviors, their futures would indeed be limited. This song encourages us as educators to look beyond the behaviors of here and now, and to allow kids to keep their dreams alive.

—Monte

Staff Development Ideas by Rick Wormeli

The Focus

In today's urgent and busy teaching world, it's easy to get complacent. Teachers do it out of survival: they're caught up in so many competing factors in daily jobs. Out of necessity they subordinate some things, unfortunately sometimes the most important ones—the growing humans they've agreed to teach. If teachers are not diligent, each student can become one more paper to grade, another chair in the row, or another mess to clean up amidst a sea of everyday commitments. Students may enter a teacher's consciousness only superficially. Arbitrary impressions and labels encourage teachers to fit individual students into a preconceived schema for who they are and who they will become. These impressions are frequently inaccurate.

The Song

"Armstrong" is a plea from a middle school child to shake teachers out of complacency. The verses urge teachers to look closely to see the real person inside him and to guide him to greatness. It is particularly powerful in that the student who is making his case for becoming something special is completely average. Listen to one message in the lyrics: Many students and teachers are wrapped in plain-brown wrappers, but when teachers extend themselves to see the depth, complexities, and talents within, the students unwrapped are capable of tremendous feats of courage, contribution, and creativity. A good teacher is about more than just taking attendance and distributing No. 2 pencils, and Armstrong hopes for such a teacher every year.

A second message is among the most poignant: Being a young adolescent means being perpetually in contrast. At this age, individuals want to belong and to be separate; to label others and be labeled, but not to be limited to the labels; individuals are immortal and mortal in the space of sixty seconds, and they want to take bold steps, as long as someone else leads the way.

Despite the student in the song's aloof nature and average-ness, he declares that he is unique, worthy of a teacher's dedication. He looks to his teacher for assurance that his hope is justified. He asks his teachers to look past who he is now to what he will become. In short, he asks to be inspired so that he can achieve the heights of personal performance: to stand where Armstrong—Neil or Lance—stood.

The Hook

It's the first day of school. You greet your students at the door to the classroom. As they enter, one child—an average-looking individual—seems to be ready to ask you a question.

Armstrong

I take out the trash, pick up my socks,
Put down the lid, and don't forget
    to wash.
Where do I begin?
Walking the dog, talking online,
Lacing my shoes, it takes too
    much time;
I'm late again.
Racing across my neighbor's yard
For a pick-up game with the guys
    in the park
Might seem like I'm just
    your average kid . . .

CHORUS:
    But, help me stand where
        Armstrong stood,
    To live the dreams that fill my mind.
    Hear the future in my voice,
    Guide my steps for all mankind.
    Push me out beyond what's known,
    Let me use it all for good—
    Help me stand,
    Help me stand where
        Armstrong stood

I love to paint, and I can do math,
Tell a good joke, and make
    people laugh,
But I'm scared of war.
Reading my books, raising my hand,
Daring to hope,
Someone understands.
Don't look at my test scores.
And I'm not the tallest on the ball team,
In marching band I play tambourine,
I may not look like a superstar—

CHORUS:
    But, help me stand where
        Armstrong stood,
    To live the dreams that fill my mind.
    Hear the future in my voice,
    Guide my steps for all mankind.
    Push me out beyond what's known,
    Let me use it all for good—
    Help me stand,
    Help me stand where
        Armstrong stood.

I'm Picasso, I'm James Dean,
    Dr. Martin Luther King.
I am Einstein, I'm the one and only me—

CHORUS:
    Please help me stand where
        Armstrong stood,
    To live the dreams that fill my mind.
    Hear the future in my voice,
    Guide my steps for all mankind,
    Push me out beyond what's known,
    Let me use it all for good.
    Help me stand,
    Help me stand,
    Help me stand,
    Help me stand where
        Armstrong stood.
    Oh, help me stand.

– Monte Selby and Rick Wormeli
©2004 Street Singer Music, BMI/
Toto Tunes, ASCAP

> ## Activity for a Large Group

Recognizing What Lies Within

Purpose:

- To help teachers look beyond the surface behaviors and features students present to them
- To help teachers keep in mind the depth and diversity of the students they teach

Materials:

- Large drawing paper
- Colored marking pens
- Masking tape or adhesive

Step-by-step:

1. In small groups, ask teachers to draw a typical middle school kid, identifying five or more external characteristics that portray the student's membership in his or her peer group. This can include clothing, accessories, carry-able property, hairstyles, attitudes, gestures, and anything else that students would adorn or display in order to be acceptable to their peers. No more than seven minutes should be allotted to this task.

2. Ask each group to create five or more caption bubbles near the student's head on its drawing. Inside each bubble, record internal monologue comments that reveal the student's thoughts—unique concerns, ponderings, talents, dreams (goals), and hopes—that belie those outer characteristics.

   > *For example: A male student with an iPod earphone stuck in his ear might seem like he is distancing himself from others, wanting to lose himself in his hip-hop music, but he has caption bubbles that say, "I wonder if anyone knows I write poetry," "If I act like I'm listening to my iPod, maybe nobody will ask me anything and realize how much I don't know," or "This song has a great sound, but I'm not sure I believe what the words say I should believe." Allow up to seven minutes for these caption bubbles.*

3. Once the drawings are complete and if time allows, ask each group to share them with the larger group.

4. As a large group, respond to as many of the following questions as time allows:

- What do we see on the outside of our middle school students on a daily basis?

- What are some of the untapped talents and gifts that lie within our students?

- How do good teachers see through the negative or apathetic façades some students present to us and instead find the positive potential that lies inside each one?

- How do we enable students to identify their own unique gifts and talents, particularly when they don't see these gifts and talents in themselves?

- What are some of the unspoken worries/concerns of our students?

- How do we enable students to share their unspoken worries/concerns without being intrusive to their lives?

- How do we help students deal with their worries/concerns constructively?

- How can we as teachers keep from becoming complacent regarding our students' individual gifts/talents/dreams/ponderings/worries/hopes?

- Is any of this beyond the classroom teacher's role? Are we only to deliver the curriculum, or are we also to help with students' personal development as an individual and citizen? Explain.

Activities for a Small Group

Being a Trusted Steward of Students

Purpose:

- To help teachers recognize what they do as they coach students through their academic years

- To provide an inclination and structure for looking past students' outward appearance and behavior to what lies within

Materials:

Copies of "September Plea" (page 39)

Step-by-step:

1. Read the poem "September Plea," which was the catalyst for the lyrics that later became the song "Armstrong."

2. Brainstorm for a moment individually about what makes for a high-quality, trusted steward of students' development. List responses in a bulleted list. If folks need suggestions to get started, consider using: attentiveness, forgiveness, moral/ethical behavior, hope, vision, courage, and a sense of humor.

3. Ask each member of the group to share his or her brainstormed thinking.

4. As a group, identify the three most important characteristics of a trusted steward of students' development.

5. Finally, ask each member of the group to identify one aspect of their teaching that exemplifies each of these three characteristics. If someone is having trouble identifying something they do that expresses one or more of these characteristics, brainstorm possibilities with that individual. Sometimes we can't see our own positive behaviors objectively, and our colleagues can help.

Share What Lies Within You

Purpose:

- To encourage teachers to look below the surface and recognize their colleagues' hidden talents and gifts
- To recognize students for their *Armstrong-like* accomplishments

Materials:

Step-by-step:

1. Have teachers share the talents and gifts that colleagues might not get to see unless they knew you outside of school. For example, some of us are champion quilters, golfers, guitarists, and scuba divers, and others have successfully resolved major labor disputes or studied abroad. Some of us have written books, and some could rival chef Emeril with exemplary cooking. Some of us did remarkable things in our youth—both positive and not so positive—that we might be comfortable sharing with our colleagues. One educator I know is a teacher during the week, a pastor on the weekends, and an award-winning hockey goalie in the winter.

2. Once everyone has finished sharing, identify current and former middle school students who surprised you with their background or talents.

3. Choose one student who presented himself or herself initially as average or somewhat less than stellar, but later revealed a depth or talent that indicated there was much more to this person than met the eye. For example:

I've taught an academically and socially average seventh-grader who raised $22,000 in one day for the Juvenile Diabetes Foundation. He is diabetic himself, so it was particularly meaningful. Another seventh-grader was extremely shy in class discussions, but sang opera at the Kennedy Center in Washington, D.C., every year. One student wrote two grade levels below his current grade level, yet repeatedly won forensic debate contests with his quick thinking and oratory gift. Another student had spoken so little during the first three months of school, most of our team couldn't remember what her voice sounded like in early December, yet she later coordinated the printing and distribution of the school's literary magazine to local businesses in our community. Still another middle school student was severely learning disabled and had Tourette's syndrome, yet earned the lead in Romeo and Juliet and performed the two-hour show without a single misstep or tic.

4. Finally, brainstorm as a group how teachers can remain diligent in finding these hidden depths and talents within every student, not just a few throughout the year, and not just in the "get-to-know-you" activities early in the year.

5. As a last step, ask each member of the group to give serious attention to one or more of the average students in his or her classes over the next two weeks, and to report to the rest of the group about at least one previously unknown talent or gift discovered in one of those students.

Activity for Individuals

Fulfilling Our Dreams

Purpose:

- To help teachers empathize with students' goals for themselves
- To help teachers identify the specific strategies they can impart to students to help attain their goals
- To inspire teachers to reexamine their role as something more than just a purveyor of academics and skills

Armstrong

Materials:

- Journal or computer
- Pen or pencil or computer paper

Step-by-step:

1. Reflect and journal for a few minutes in response to the following prompt:

   Recall your days as a student. Try to recall your dreams for yourself. Include your early career choices, desired achievements, and hopes. Record at least three of these.

2. Then, identify which dreams you achieved, and more importantly, what it was that enabled you to achieve them.

3. Read over what you have written. How would you be different if you had not achieved your dreams or goals? Identify at least two differences.

4. Finally, *connect your personal experience with your classroom.* Respond to these questions:

   - What is sacrificed when we do not see the potential inside individual students?
   - Does the classroom experience we provide enable the Picasso, James Dean, Martin Luther King, Einstein, and comparable figures in each child to manifest themselves? Why or why not, and if not, how can we change our classrooms?

Additional Questions to Consider in the Large Group, Small Group, or by Yourself

- What do we sacrifice if a child isn't taught to advocate for himself or to be fully individual?

- How have students had a chance to define themselves in my class this week?

- How can we get students to individualize (put their own spins or styles into) their responses to our prompts and teaching?

- How do we avoid stereotyping students?

- What are the stereotypes we present to students every day unknowingly?

September Plea

Hey, you up there at the front of the room,
The one I see past spiral notebooks and eraser filings,
Under the taunting clock next to the question of the day,
While dreaming of brown-haired Melissa,
Or staring at pages on which I'm supposed to read along silently as you read aloud,
Here it is:

At the end of our time together,
It doesn't matter what you taught.
I am not here to fill a seat
Or give you a place to go each morning.

What matters is what I take with me after
    being with you.
I am here to master all you have to offer,
Not skim smooth and round across
    flat water.
I'm here to dive deeply,
To belong to something larger
    than myself,
To marvel at questions I didn't know existed,
And to gulp competence.

Please don't settle for mediocrity,
Don't turn to the next page of the textbook
Because it's the next page of the textbook.
Don't limit me to your creativity,
Trust me to find connections
    you don't see.

Fight those who would use me
    as the canary in the cage,
Judging society's health on whether or
    not I maintain my perch.
Someone who pushes on the
    mall Santa's belly
In hopes that one day the wedged pillow
    might be flesh and Santa real,
Shouldn't be society's yardstick.

Just remember what is was like to be me,
When the future was wide open,
    anything you desired.
Then build it —
With every word you say,
Every lesson you plan,
Every hallway you walk,
Every pencil you loan.

Teach me to be a trusted guardian
Of all that is worth keeping.
Be my steward.

What page are we on again?

– **Rick Wormeli, from *Day One and Beyond*,
published by Stenhouse Publishers, 2003.
Used with permission.**

Look Me in the Eye

The Story Behind the Song

When I was the principal of Felten Middle School in Hays, Kansas, Mark Massaglia was our teacher for multigrade level drama courses. Drama became so popular we quadrupled the number of classes offered. Mark found himself with three nonverbal students in wheelchairs who wanted to participate in the drama program. Mark wrote a play in which the three were the star characters, and asked me to write a song to support the content of the play. The production was an instant success with the local community. The young actors even traveled to Topeka to present their play to an audience that included influential legislators. Think about it—what would you want to say if you couldn't speak?

—Monte

Staff Development Ideas by Kathy Hunt-Ullock

The Focus

"Look Me in the Eye" and its activities are designed to remind teachers that students with disabilities have a profound need to belong, to be appreciated, to be acknowledged, and to be treated just like the other students.

The Song

The song, written for and inspired by Mark Massaglia's original one-act play of the same name, was originally performed by Felton Middle School students and had a profound impact on their acceptance of students with disabilities within the drama program at Felton. The play's message regarding disabilities was unforgettable to the students as well as to the community members who viewed the play!

The Hook

Do you have a staff member who uses a wheelchair or special hearing aids and glasses? Has a staff member ever suffered an injury that limited his or her mobility? How did each of these teachers deal with their *disabilities*? Ask participants to share personal experiences. What were the circumstances? What problems did they have? How did they alter their behavior in order to function well? How did it feel? Do you have students with disabilities who must find ways to deal with the everyday challenges of the school day? Think about those students.

Look Me in the Eye

I've been sitting here looking at you
You've been standing there looking away
In this wheelchair my legs won't move
You avoid me, don't know what to say
Come on, it ain't wrong

> CHORUS: Look me in the eye
> Open your heart
> There's so much to see
> Come on think it over
> It's all right to look a little closer, at me

Don't you wonder if we agree
On what makes us happy or angry?
So much in common, so much to lose
When we keep that distance between me and you
Come on, it ain't wrong

> CHORUS: Look me in the eye
> Open your heart
> There's so much to see
> Come on think it over
> It's all right to look a little closer, at me

I know this isn't easy
Friendship's a two-way street
But there's so much we can offer
Making us more complete

> CHORUS: Look me in the eye
> Open your heart
> There's so much to see
> In you and me
> Come on think it over
> It's all right to look a little closer, at me

Activities for a Large Group

Out of Purse or Pocket

Purpose:

> To encourage individuals to think seriously about the importance of teamwork in compensating for the loss of important items used in everyday activities

Materials:

- Items from participants' purses or pockets
- Pencils and paper

Step-by-step:

1. Divide participants into groups of four or five. Each group should select a recorder. The recorder will need a piece of paper and a pencil.

2. Have group members go into their purses, pockets, or briefcases and take out two important items, placing them so that others in the group can see the items. The items should be things the individuals have with them daily. Participants may take items off their bodies such as shoes, jewelry, etc.

3. Without telling the group what they will be doing with the items, have them select three items as most important to their group. The rest of the items can now be pushed aside.

4. Have each group imagine that the three items they have chosen are no longer accessible. The members of the group must live and function without the three items. Ask them to think about how their lives would be changed and how they would compensate for the loss of each item—their "disability." The recorder should record the responses in three lists. Give the groups approximately ten minutes to complete their discussion.

5. If time permits, have groups share the results of their discussions. Losing the use of a key or a favorite pen results in inconvenience and, in some cases, requires creative problem solving. Ask if the discussion required working together to compensate for the loss of their items.

6. Have participants imagine that instead losing of the use of a key or some other item participants selected, they lost the use of their eyes or their legs. Emphasize the need to work together to come up with creative ways to help each other, to encourage each other, to understand each other, and to "Look Each Other in the Eye."

Tootsie Roll Pop Groups

Purpose:

To encourage participants to look beyond individual differences
to find common attributes

Materials:

- Tootsie Roll Pops
- Paper and pencils

Step-by-step:

1. Have Tootsie Roll Pops available in lots of different colors. As people are entering the room, have them pick a Tootsie Roll Pop and be seated. After hearing Monte's song, ask people to form groups of four or five people with the same color Tootsie Roll Pop. Number each group as they are working.

2. Make the following statement to the groups:

   When you identify with someone because of a similarity, you are more likely to like that person. If you focus only on other peoples' differences, the differences will be more important than if you consider the differences in combination with their similarities. Here's to what we have in common and not to what divides us.

3. The person in each group with the most blue-colored clothing becomes the group facilitator and assigns a recorder. The recorder of each group is then given a piece of paper and a pencil.

4. The group must now find four unusual common group attributes. For example, if the group states that they all teach in the same school, that is not unusual. Examples of attributes that might be considered unusual are: all have been to Europe, all have pierced ears, all have been in a car accident, all have been married more than once, all hate anchovies, etc. Give the groups approximately eight minutes to complete their list.

5. When a group number is called, the recorder should stand and explain the four unusual attributes that the members of their group have in common. Choose as many groups to share as time allows.

6. At the end of the session, remind the participants that our similarities are the glue that helps us all work well together, no matter what our gender, age, ethnicity, disability, or religion. If the world only operated this way, what a better world we would have.

Activity for a Small Group

Human Sandwich Board

Purpose:

To point out that everyone does some things well and has trouble doing other things

Materials:

- Flip chart paper
- Masking tape
- Dark-colored marking pens

Step-by-step:

1. Give each participant TWO pieces of flip chart paper, one dark-colored marking pen, and TWO strips of masking tape, each 16" long. Explain that each person will be creating a personal sandwich board.

2. On one piece of chart paper, participants will list three things that they do well, and on the other piece of paper they will list three things that they have trouble doing, or in other words, three things that they would consider "disabilities." Give participants approximately five minutes to create their lists.

3. Once both lists are created, participants should place their "ability" list on their chest and their "disability" list on their back. The strips should be placed over each shoulder to act as straps, securing the flip chart paper in place like a sandwich board.

4. When the sandwich boards are in place, divide the group in half. The two groups form concentric circles. The people in the inside circle should be facing outward, while the people in the outside circle should be facing inward. Line up the circles so that each person from the inside circle is facing a person from the outside circle.

5. Participants in the outside circle share their front and back posters with their partners, then the individuals in the inside circle should do the same. Allow about one minute for the pair to share. When the time is up, ring a bell, sound a buzzer, flip the lights, etc., and ask the inside circle to move a certain number of spots clockwise. Then start the

sharing again in the same manner as described above. Allow as many pairs to share as time allows.

6. End the session by stating that all of us have disabilities. Some are temporary, some are permanent, some are easy to see, some are hidden, some are severe, and some are mild. We are all in this together and we should all work together to make everyone feel welcome, valued, and appreciated.

Activity for Individuals

Knowing What to Do

Purpose:

- To develop a personal set of guidelines for interacting with people with disabilities

- To encourage teachers to consider how everyday interactions are perceived by those with disabilities

Materials:

- Copies of "Positive Interactions" (pages 48 and 49)

- Paper and pencil

Step-by-step:

1. Distribute the "Positive Interactions" information sheets.

2. Think about the way you would want to be treated as a person with a disability.

3. Develop a personal set of guidelines to use for interacting with people with disabilities.

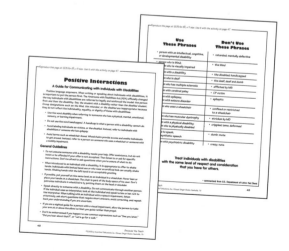

Positive Interactions

A Guide for Communicating with Individuals with Disabilities

Positive language empowers. When writing or speaking about individuals with disabilities, it is important to put the person first. The *Americans with Disabilities Act* (ADA) officially changed the way individuals with disabilities are referred to legally and reinforced the model: the person first and then the disability. Say *the student with a disability* rather than *the disabled student*. Group designations such as *the blind*, *the retarded*, or *the disabled* are inappropriate because they do not reflect the individuality, equality, or dignity of those with disabilities.

- Use the word *disability* when referring to someone who has a physical, mental, emotional, sensory, or learning impairment.

- Do not use the word *handicapped*. A handicap is what a person with a disability cannot do.

- Avoid labeling individuals as *victims*, or *the disabled*. Instead, refer to *individuals with disabilities* or *someone who has epilepsy*.

- Avoid terms such as *wheelchair-bound*. Wheelchairs provide access and enable individuals to get around. Instead, refer to a person as *someone who uses a wheelchair* or *someone with a mobility impairment*.

General Guidelines

- Do not assume someone with a disability needs your help. Offer assistance, but do not insist or be offended if your offer is not accepted. Then listen to or ask for specific instructions. Don't be afraid to ask questions when you're unsure of what to do.

- When introduced to an individual with a disability, it is appropriate to offer to shake hands. Individuals with limited hand use or who wear an artificial limb can usually shake hands. Shaking hands with the left hand is an acceptable greeting.

- If possible, put yourself at the same level as an individual in a wheelchair. Never lean or place your hands on a wheelchair. The chair is part of the body space of its user. Don't patronize individuals in wheelchairs by patting them on the head or shoulder.

- Speak directly to someone with a disability. Do not communicate through another person. If the individual uses an interpreter, look at the individual and speak to him or her, not to the interpreter. When talking with an individual with a speech impairment, listen attentively, ask short questions that require short answers, avoid correcting, and repeat back your understanding if you are uncertain.

- If you are a sighted guide for a person with a visual impairment, allow the person to take your arm at or above the elbow so that you guide rather than propel.

- Don't be embarrassed if you happen to use common expressions such as "See you later," "Did you hear about that?", or "Let's go for a walk."

Use These Phrases	Don't Use These Phrases
• person with an intellectual, cognitive, or developmental disability	• retarded; mentally defective
• person who is blind; person who is visually impaired	• the blind
• person with a disability	• the disabled; handicapped
• person who is deaf	• the deaf; deaf and dumb
• person who has multiple sclerosis	• afflicted by MS
• person with cerebral palsy	• CP victim
• person with epilepsy; person with seizure disorder	• epileptic
• person who uses a wheelchair	• confined or restricted to a wheelchair
• person who has muscular dystrophy	• stricken by MD
• person with a physical disability; person who is physically disabled	• crippled; lame; deformed
• unable to speak; uses synthetic speech	• dumb; mute
• person with psychiatric disability	• crazy; nuts

Treat individuals with disabilities with the same level of respect and consideration that you have for others.

— summarized from U.S. Department of Labor Fact Sheet

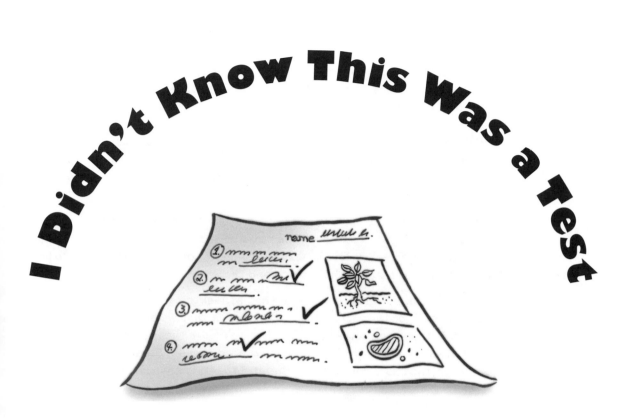

I Didn't Know This Was a Test

The Story Behind the Song

I wrote this song with Gary Cotton. Gary is a professional songwriter, a great dad, and granddad. He is thoughtful and interested in the success of all children. He says that this is the song he always wanted to write. The song is all about listening to yourself—in school and in life. You can't try hard just when it's a test—you've got to be ready all the time, 'cause you never know when it's going to count!

—Monte

Staff Development Ideas by Rick Wormeli

The Focus

How many times have we had students tell us that they didn't know something counted for their grade, and if they had, they would have worked harder on it? In most cases, students don't try to cut corners. They try to do 100% of what they are capable of doing every time they work. They don't consciously sit there and rationalize, "I'll only work to 62% of my capacity today." True, they might achieve more if they had put more effort into study, but they didn't for whatever reasons: lack of sleep, unclear expectations, low blood sugar, angst, poverty issues, cognitive development, poor communication, yelling parents, moodiness, dehydration, little exercise, no "big picture" awareness of the consequences, and/or emotional immaturity.

On the flip side, how many times have we had teachers who surprised us with a pop quiz or assessment without telling us in advance? The panic pervades every pore, and we slide lower in our seats, readying ourselves for the embarrassing lack of preparation about to be revealed. Later, we resent the teacher, the subject, and the world.

Assessment expert Rick Stiggins reminds us that students can hit any target they can see and that sits still for them. Stephen R. Covey says that we should always begin with the end in mind. Both are correct, especially when we realize that very few aspects of assessment and grading are helpful when served as surprise. Clear and frequent communication of expectations is not just nice; it's vital to student success.

The Song

While it is regrettable that some teachers play games with students by being purposefully or inadvertently coy with whether or not something counts for a grade, the teacher in the song who does this has a powerful message for students and many adults: we should do our best with all we attempt because it's a classy thing to do, and because we don't want to live to regret our actions. We want to move students toward maturity, pushing them to go that extra mile: to elaborate on their answers, to neatly insert the vertical axis on the chart, to edit their writing, to dive deeply—not superficially—into concepts, to clean up after themselves and others even when not reminded to do so, and to color their maps of China. The child who becomes the successful adult learns the power of extending himself and doing quality work early in his journey; accepting the minimum isn't good enough. These students aren't out to just pass; they want to excel.

The Hook

Every day in every school environment—whether it be impoverished or affluent; urban, rural, or suburban; with computers or without; with gang issues or without—students are being pushed by dedicated teachers like you. Just because we can't fathom how to structure learning so students choose to excel rather than coast, doesn't mean it can't be done. Let's explore some success stories, examine our own practice, and give it a try.

I Didn't Know This Was a Test

I walked in one morning to my history class
She handed out the homework and mine said I didn't pass
I raised my hand in anger, said, "I could have done my best"
"It's not fair, you should've told us, I didn't know this was a test!"

She said, "You better be ready 'cause you never know
When the grade's gonna count, but you learn as you go
That you have to be willing to do more than you're told
If you want to stand out from the rest
Don't catch yourself saying, "I didn't know this was a test."

At work in my office when the boss walked in
Said I'd been passed over for promotion again
He had read my proposal and was less than impressed
I said, "I know I have it in me, but I didn't know this was a test!"

He said, "You better be ready 'cause you never know
When the grade's gonna count, but you learn as you go
That you have to be willing to do more than you're told
If you want to stand out from the rest
Don't catch yourself saying, "I didn't know this was a test."

They said, "You better be ready 'cause you never know
When the grade's gonna count, but you learn as you go
That you have to be willing to do more than you're told
If you want to stand out from the rest
Don't catch yourself saying, "I didn't know this was a test."

I didn't know.
I didn't know this was a test.
Come on, baby, give me a break
Somebody, where's the answer?
I didn't know this was a test.
Who changed the rules anyway?
I didn't, I didn't know
I'm telling you the truth, man, I didn't know this was a test
I thought we were just having some fun y'all
I didn't know we were having a test.
Yeah.

– Monte Selby and Gary Cotton
©2004 Adobe Road Music BMI/
Street Singer Music, BMI

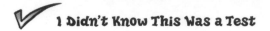

Activity for a Large Group

Are You Ready for the Test?

Purpose:

To sensitize teachers to students' test anxiety and the fairness of testing, both announced and unannounced versions

Materials:

- Small stacks of lined paper
- Copies of the fake teaching test, "TCISSDI" (page 59), or an alternative
- Pencils/pens

Step-by-step:

1. Adopt a serious disposition and explain that the state (collectively used here to reference the state, province, or political body in which the school operates) has asked that teachers be tested this week on a preselected group of topics determined by the state legislature. These tests are spot-checks to check the caliber of the teaching force within the state and to determine individual teacher salaries for next year. They were not supposed to be announced in advance. Explain that as highly accomplished professional educators, the faculty should be very comfortable in making a full and expert response to each prompt provided and in accepting the salary changes as a result of demonstrated expertise or lack thereof. Based on a teacher's response to each question, his or her salary will be adjusted higher or lower.

2. Ask everyone to take out a pen or a pencil, and distribute the exam. Explain that they will have 30 minutes to complete the entire test using the paper provided. Ask teachers to begin. Remind them to work independently of one another.

   For this fake test, consider using a math or science exam from an eighth-grade curriculum. The material on these exams is usually recognizable, though not always retrievable by most citizens. It's the kind of information listed as important for all citizens to know by legislators and the public, but few actually remember it clearly, and most feel guilty in their ignorance.

Another option for the fake test is to use the one provided at the end of this lesson. It asks general questions about the teaching profession.

3. Once teachers have had a chance to look over the questions and maybe even get a bit nervous about them, ask the staff to pause and answer the following questions:

- How are you feeling right now?

- Would this test be a fair thing to ask you to do?

- Would the results be an accurate indicator of what you know about each of these topics?

- Would the state get the data on your expertise that it needed?

- If I had told you two weeks ago that we were doing this today, what would you have changed in your life prior to coming here today at this time?

- How comfortable are you having your future salary predicated on the results of your performance on this one snapshot, 30-minute, surprise exam?

- How would you advise students facing a similar situation in their classroom studies?

- How can we help students cope with test preparation and with responding to surprise assessments?

Activity for a Small Group

Challenging Conventions in Testing

Purpose:

To sensitize teachers regarding conventional practices in testing that may or may not be effective, to enable teachers to hear the thinking of their colleagues and to exchange ideas on a critical aspect of successful teaching—assessment

Materials:

Tables or groupings of chairs so that small groups can sit and face each other in informal yet professional conversation

Step-by-step:

1. Place teachers in small groups determined by subject matter taught.

2. Ask teachers, as a group, to respond to as many of the following questions as possible:

   • What roles do pop (unannounced) quizzes and tests play in our instruction? Are they pedagogically sound practices? What do we learn about students' mastery from unannounced assessments that we don't get from previously announced assessments? How much should pop quizzes and assessments count in the overall academic grade for the grading period?

   • Do we sometimes get lost in a "gotcha" mentality when we catch students' mistakes and point those mistakes out to them? In this mode, we think that making students aware of how they've failed at something is all we have to do to teach them how to do that something better. Is this appropriate?

   • Do you agree with the statement, "The real goal of assessment is to provide instructive and constructive feedback, and to use that information to help students relearn and master the material"?
   Consider this quote:
   > *"Too often, educational tests, grades, and report cards are treated by teachers as autopsies when they should be viewed as physicals."*
   > — *Doug Reeves, author and assessment expert*

   • What would tests look like if they were more of a physical exam assessment type designed to measure and promote physical well-being?

   • What would happen if we gave students a copy of the unit test on the first day of the unit of study and allowed them to keep and reference it for the duration of the unit?

   • Forced-choice questions and prompts require students to choose from responses provided by the teacher such as true/false, matching, and multiple-choice items. The student does not have to generate the information.

- Constructed-response questions and prompts ask students to generate and apply information themselves. Examples of constructed responses include: opportunities to interpret graphs, short essays, short answer, drawings, making analogies, mind maps, and flowcharts. Teachers may feel more comfortable with one format over another if they were to give the test out ahead of time.

> ♪ Note to teacher-leader or principal: You may have to explain that there are two types of tests: forced-choice and constructed-response.

- How would providing the test ahead of time change our teaching?

- What is the goal of a test? What classroom practices reveal an accurate and fair rendering of students' achievement of that goal? What might impede that goal?

3. Have each group identify eight helpful test-preparation strategies students could be taught. Remember, it is a waste of our planet's oxygen to tell most students, "Study for tomorrow's test." They don't know how or they don't have the self-discipline to do a thorough job. Most students require an assigned set of steps for reviewing material.

Activity for Individuals

Getting Students to Extend Themselves

Purpose:

To give teachers the time and inclination to create specific lessons that help students learn the importance of achieving excellence, not just getting by

Materials:

- Paper
- Time to work independently

Step-by-step:

1. Ask teachers to design a specific three-lesson experience of whatever length is appropriate for the students they teach. The experience must enable students to learn the importance of going the extra mile in their work. These don't have to be

formal lesson plans, just a description of the important learning experience they would provide. Evidence of the success of the lessons would be that students would choose on their own to demonstrate pride in their work, concerned enough about the quality that they would take actions such as:

- Revising poorly worded sections of text
- Taking notes on something about which you did not ask them to take notes
- Coloring something to make it more attractive
- Creating their own personal study sheet or card of the testable information
- Finding a second source to verify something, not just settle for the one they find
- Responding to their opposition's arguments in a debate or persuasive essay before their opposition can make them
- Picking up trash
- Organizing a messy area
- Using a ruler for drawing graphs
- Double-checking their math problem solutions
- Studying for a test beyond just reading the material
- Getting supplies together soon enough to complete a project
- Creating a calendar of completion to finish a project
- Asking for help early in the learning process if they are struggling

2. With teachers' permission, post these strategies for the whole faculty to consider and ask that teachers give permission for others to use their ideas.

T C I S S D I

Teacher Caliber Inferential Sampling and Salary Determinant Inventory

Teacher: _____   Grade Level(s): _____

School: _____   Years as a Teacher: _____

On a separate sheet of paper, respond to each prompt completely:

1. Describe Vygotsky's *Zone of Proximal Development* and provide two different examples of its application in your classroom practice from the past four weeks of teaching. Finally, explain what role Tomlinson's "Ratcheting" has in working with students' zones of proximal development.

2. Explain how the Primacy-Recency Effect supports Daily Oral Language, Warm-up, or "Early Bird" exercises that students do as they first enter a teacher's classroom.

3. Identify three major contributions to learning theory made by Jerome Bruner.

4. Explain at least three roles of assessment in a developmentally appropriate instructional program.

5. Choose any one of the following topics and identify at least three strategies a highly accomplished teacher would employ to teach it to his or her students:
   - Lunar phases
   - Chromatic scale
   - Writer's voice
   - Photosynthesis
   - The role of stretching when we exercise
   - The use of line and shading to evoke emotion
   - The impact of railroads on westward expansion
   - The rise of city-states in Mesopotamia
   - Designing a Website
   - Adding fractions
   - Graphing inequalities
   - Poetic devices

6. In the Supreme Court's 1988 case, *Hazelwood School District v. Kuhlmeier*, did the right of a school board to regulate student expression include teacher expression as well? What constitutes a legitimate pedagogical interest according to Hazelwood, and can a school board still discipline a student and/or a teacher if she cannot articulate one for a given situation?

7. Under *No Child Left Behind* Legislation, what is AYP and what happens to schools that don't make it after two years? after three years?

8. Our administration supports the teaching of reading across the content areas. Describe three reading strategies you've promoted this year with your students that will help them improve their reading in the content areas.

9. A teacher asks his students to infer an author's meaning or make an inference based on scientific or historical data. What specific skills must students have in order to make inferences? List at least five.

10. Which grading scale is a more accurate portrayal of a student's mastery of a subject over time: 100-point or 4-point? Support your answer with specific examples from your classroom practice this year and cite at least one research source that supports your position.

Beat of a Different Marcher

The Story Behind the Song

Debbie Silver and I wrote this song after discussing her book *Drumming to the Beat of Different Marchers*. We rewrote it several times before we found the magic in the words. This song could be the theme song for differentiated instruction. It speaks to every educator and reminds them that all children are within reach. It is up to us to find their rhythm.

—Monte

Staff Development Ideas by Debbie Silver

The Focus

To help teachers appreciate the importance of finding the strengths within every student and giving them a reasonable chance at success.

The Song

Monte and Debbie's song is a celebration of the unique differences in students. It urges educators to "hear the voice" of every learner. Printed lyrics should be given to teachers before the song is played, as the words move fast.

The Activities

Facilitators ask participants to jot a quick list of the "different marchers" they are currently teaching and what methods they have tried so far to reach those learners. In both large group activities, participants face the challenge of finding differences in groups that seem to be about the same. Each activity can be used as a natural "stepping stone" to conversations about why differentiated instruction is important and worthwhile.

In the small group activities, members can experience firsthand how if feels to hear "a different drummer." The paper-folding activity demonstrates that perceptions vary according to the learner.

The first individual activity for this unit is designed to provide teachers with a first step toward differentiating instruction, assignments, and assessments. In the second activity, participants are asked to generate ideas to overcome obstacles in implementing differentiated instruction. And in the third follow-up, they are asked to think deeply about their responsibilities to students as individuals.

The Hook

As you listen to this song, think about the different learners that walk, dash, meander, slink, or stride into your classroom every day.

Beat of a Different Marcher

Bobby marches to the beat
    of his different drummers
Jeffery does his reading,
    but he can't do numbers
Shawna's up and talkin'
    90 miles an hour, again
Can't find his book or pencil,
    that would be Ben.

Hyperactive, dyslexic,
    class clown, non-reader
Upper class, no class,
    off-task, bottom feeder
Little Arty's a challenge;
    Martin's a dream
We've seen them all, they all
    need to be seen.

All children in reach
    when we find their rhythm —
The step, the dance,
    the song within them
That's a better journey,
    but so much harder
Too extraordinary, but so much smarter
To drum to the beat
    of each different marcher.

Sandy's in the slow group,
    a proven low achiever
She's the small quiet one,
    not a class leader
Crayons in her hand,
    she can draw what she knows best
But no room for pictures
    on the standardized test.

Ballerina, bricklayer,
    biochemist, ball player
Diesel driver, drum major,
    diva-destined, dragonslayer —
Some kids have a chance,
    with a different choice
To show what they know,
    they must have a voice.

All children in reach
    when we find their rhythm —
The step, the dance,
    the song within them
That's a better journey,
    but so much harder
Too extraordinary, but so much smarter
To drum to the beat
    of each different marcher.

Introspective, oversized,
    minimized, criticized
Round holes, square lives,
    not much room for compromise.
There's a new song not yet written
For each and every child, will we listen?

All children in reach
    when we find their rhythm—
The step, the dance, the song within them
That's a better journey,
    but so much harder
Too extraordinary, but so much smarter
To drum to the beat
    of each different marcher.
Let's all dance to the beat
    of each different marcher!

– Monte Selby & Debbie Silver
©2002 Street Singer Music, BMI/Toto Tunes, ASCAP

Activities for a Large Group

Recognizing Differences

Purpose:

- To introduce the concept of differentiation
- To begin a discussion on the importance of using differences in students to their advantage

Materials:

- Basket of lemons—one lemon per participant
- Table for displaying the lemons

Step-by-step:

In this activity, lemons are used to illustrate a few important points about individual differences.

1. Hand out a lemon to every participant. Tell each person to take a little time to really study her/his lemon. Ask each person to examine it, get to know it, and take time to "bond" with it. (That should bring a laugh.) Stress that it is important that each participant truly know his or her own lemon.

2. Have someone collect all the lemons in a box or basket. Mix them up. Spread all the lemons on a table at the front of the room. Ask participants to come up and pick up their personal lemons and take them back to their seats. (If there is some disagreement about who owns a particular lemon, try to help them sort out the problem.)

3. When all participants have retrieved their lemons, ask the audience, "How did you know which lemon was yours?" "How sure are you that you have the correct lemon?"

4. Discuss the fact that even though all the lemons were roughly the same size and color, there were distinct differences if one looked closely enough.

5. Help the audience members apply the analogy to students. Ask them to discuss the importance of recognizing differences in our students. You may point out that even when something is labeled "a lemon," it has its own unique and important traits.

I Can Do Something!

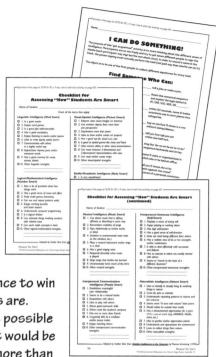

Purpose:

- To remind teachers that every individual has different strengths and weaknesses

- To review the concepts of multiple intelligences

Materials:

- copies of "I Can Do Something!" (page 72)

- copies of "Checklist for Assessing 'How' Students Are Smart" (pages 73 and 74)

- Small prizes

Step-by-step:

1. Tell the participants they are going to have a chance to win "fabulous" prizes. Do not disclose what the prizes are. Explain that each person is to read over the eight possible tasks and sign her/his own name by one task that would be easy to do. (Even though they may be able to do more than one task, they should pick only the task easiest for them to do.)

2. After signing their own sheets, participants begin moving around, collecting signatures from others who can perform the remaining tasks.

3. Emphasize that it is not acceptable for a person just to say he or she can perform a task, the person must actually do the task before signing another person's sheet. Every task must have a different signature so that in the end there are eight different signatures on the paper.

4. As soon as one collects eight different signatures, she or he shows the completed sheet to the facilitator and collects a prize. (Keep the prizes small and fun so that the focus is on the process and not the incentive.)

5. After awarding a few prizes, give a signal that all prizes have been awarded and have participants return to their seats.

6. Debrief the activity by asking participants if they found a variety of strengths among their peers. Point out that even though one may or may not be able to do one thing does not necessarily indicate a strength or lack of it in a particular intelligence. A strength can be validated by having several indicators for it.

7. Hand out copies of the checklists. Explain that being able to check off several items in a category usually indicates a strength for that particular intelligence.

Ask audience members if they have already made such observations about their students. If not, the checklist is a good place to start. (If the checklist is not age-appropriate for the participant's students, urge them to find or write a modified version to use with their classes.)

8. Discuss why it might be beneficial to know the main strengths of every student. Ask teachers what kinds of decisions they can make based on this information. Ask them what else is important to know about every student in the classroom.

Activities for a Small Group

Hearing a Different Drummer

Purpose:

- To help participants observe how people's perceptions are not always alike
- To initiate a discussion on how students learn in different ways

Materials:

One sheet of copy paper for each participant

Step-by-step:

1. Hand out one sheet of copy paper to each participant and ask everyone to listen closely and follow your directions precisely.
   Give these directions:
   - Hold your sheet of paper in front of you with both hands.
   - Close your eyes, and do not open them again until I ask you to.
     Follow my exact directions, but ask no questions.
     Do not say anything until I ask you to open your eyes.
   - Fold your paper in half. *(Pause)*
   - Fold your paper in half again. *(Pause)*
   - Fold your paper in half again. *(Pause)*
   - Tear off the right-hand corner. *(Pause)*
   - Turn your paper over. *(Pause)*
   - Tear off the left-hand corner. *(Pause)*
   - Unfold your sheet of paper, and hold it in front of you. *(Pause)*
   - Please open your eyes.

2. It will be immediately obvious that everyone does not have the same finished product. Discuss how individuals create understandings for themselves in different ways.

3. Apply this demonstration to individual differences in the classroom.

What Can I Do with the Kid Who . . . ?

Purpose:

-   To brainstorm ideas for students with particular learning needs
-   To practice adding levels of support to give students a reasonable chance for success

Materials:

-   Chart paper
-   Marking pens
-   Copies of the "Practice Examples" (page 75)
-   Various teacher resources

Step-by-step:

1. Invite the group to participate in planning some differentiated instruction, assignments, and assessments together. Teachers can bring actual lessons to the session with specific students in mind, or they can begin by using generalized practice examples (see page 75).

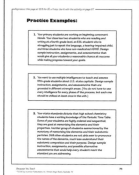

2. Have each group choose a recorder. As in all good brainstorming sessions, ideas should flow freely, and should not be critiqued or edited until the end.

3. Once a critical mass of ideas has been generated, the group works together to outline a realistic, standards-based lesson that embraces many kinds of learners.

Differentiation Through Centers

Purpose:
- To encourage teachers to use centers to help differentiate instruction
- To generate ideas for centers that appeal to multiple intelligences

Materials:
- Chart paper
- Markers

Step-by-step:

1. Explain that research tells us that all age groups (even secondary students) benefit from the reinforcement offered by effective learning centers. Learning centers can include workstations around the classroom that focus on different methods and/or goals. In this activity, teachers brainstorm ideas for centers in their classroom that can be used to introduce, instruct, or extend knowledge in a certain subject area.

2. Remind teachers that a learning "center" can be any designated area in the classroom—a computer, a table, an interactive bulletin board, a floor mat, etc.

3. Tell them they are going to work together to create eight possible learning centers based on Howard Gardner's eight levels of intelligence.
   The desired outcome is for all students to be able to find the volume of a cube, a cone, and a cylinder. The goal is not for students merely to memorize formulas, but for them to be able to solve authentic problems using the essential ideas of finding the volume of a three-dimensional object.

4. Brainstorm ideas for each of these levels of intelligence:

   Linguistic (word smart)—

   Logical-mathematical (number smart)—

   Naturalist (nature smart)—

   Bodily-kinesthetic (body smart)—

   Musical (music smart)—

   Visual-spatial (picture smart)—

   Intrapersonal Awareness (self-smart)—

   Interpersonal Communication Skills (people smart)—

Activities for Individuals

Step One

Purpose:

- To help teachers focus on important differences among learners in the classroom
- To give teachers a starting point from which to begin differentiated instruction

Materials:

5" x 8" index cards

Step-by-step:

1. Prepare a 5" x 8" index card for each student in your room. The card should include:

    - the student's name at the top
    - a place to record information such as:

        Reading level—

        English language proficiency level—

        Level of adult supervision and involvement at home—

        Areas of strengths—

        Areas of weaknesses—

        Preferred learning style—

        Personal interests—

        Least favorite things—

        Fears—

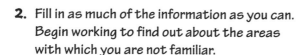

Note: Add or delete items as you see fit for your needs.

2. Fill in as much of the information as you can. Begin working to find out about the areas with which you are not familiar.

3. Update and add to the information as you learn more about the student.

4. Periodically review the information and use it to plan differentiated instruction, assignments, and assessments.

Overcoming Obstacles

Purpose:

- To overcome objections to implementing differentiated learning components
- To focus on realistic goals and strategies for implementing differentiated instruction

Materials:

- Paper or journal
- Pencil or pen

Step-by-step:

1. Make three columns on your paper.

2. In the first column make a list of all the obstacles preventing you from implementing differentiating instruction in your classroom. Write every possible objection. Be as specific as possible.

3. In the second column write a fantasy solution beside every obstacle listed in column one. Your ideas should be creative and ingenious ("in-a-perfect-world"-type answers).

4. In the third column try to think of some actual realistic, "doable" solutions to the obstacles and objections that, at the very least, could "get things started."

5. Read over your solutions in column three and highlight the ideas you generated that could be implemented now without a tremendous investment in time, resources, or other things beyond your control.

6. Choose one of your highlighted answers to work on over the next few weeks. Keep notes on your progress.

Journal Assignment—Inspiring Different Marchers

Purpose:

- To help teachers reflect on the true purpose of education
- To help teachers clarify their roles as educators

Materials:

- Journals
- Pens or pencil

Step-by-step:

1. Answer the following questions in your journal:

   A. How important is it for teachers and schools to recognize and validate multiple intelligences and varied learning styles?

   B. Do you see a disconnect between the philosophical view "students can learn but at different rates" and the current trend toward more standardized teaching and testing? Explain.

   C. How do you feel about the following statement?
   "As a classroom teacher my responsibility is to teach according to the state standards. It is up to individual students to find a way to meet the class norms and the district's expectations. That's the way it is in life, and that's the way it is in here."

2. Summarize and respond to one or more of the following quotations:

   A. "To teachers, students are the end products—all else is a means. Hence there is but one interpretation of high standards in teaching; standards are highest where the maximum number of students—slow learners and fast learners alike—develop to their maximal capacity."

   —Joseph Seidlin

   B. "The essence of education is not to stuff you with facts but to help you discover your uniqueness, to teach you how to develop it, and then to show you how to give it away."

   —Leo Buscaglia

   C. "Education should never work against a person's destiny, but should achieve the full development of his own predispositions. The education of a man today so often lags behind the talents and tendencies which his destiny has implanted in him. We must keep pace with these powers to such an extent that the human being in our care can win his way through to all that his destiny will allow—to the fullest clarity of thought, the most loving deepening of his feeling, and the greatest possible energy and ability of will. This can only be done by an art of education and teaching which is based on a real knowledge of man."

   —Rudolf Steiner

   D. "Education is not filling a bucket, but lighting a fire."

   —William Butler Yeats

Name _____

I CAN DO SOMETHING!

The purpose of this "get acquainted" activity is to start thinking about the different areas of intelligence. Participants are to mix freely and try to get seven different people to sign the blanks (each participant may sign her/his own sheet once). In order to record a name in the blank, the person signing must actually perform the task (not just say that she/he can do it).

The object is to be one of the first people to collect different signatures for every task.

Find Someone Who Can:

_____ tell a joke or make a pun.

_____ finish this numerical sequence
and explain the logic behind it:
81, 196, 100, 169, 121, _____ .

_____ within 20 seconds, name 6 traits
scientists use to sort plants into
categories.

_____ hop on one foot 3 times in a row
without losing balance.

_____ tell you how tall you are
within one-half inch.

_____ sing the "do-re-mi-fa-so-la-ti-do"
sequence backwards and on key.

_____ name 5 clubs or organizations in
which she or he held an office.

_____ tell you 5 times she or he
"went against the crowd"
because of a personal conviction.

© Debbie Silver, 2006

Because You Teach
©2006 by Incentive Publications, Inc./Street Singer Books, Nashville, TN

Checklist for
Assessing "How" Students Are Smart

Name of Student: _____

Check all the items that apply:

Linguistic Intelligence (Word Smart)

☐ 1. Is a good reader

☐ 2. Enjoys word games

☐ 3. Is a good joke teller/storyteller

☐ 4. Has a good vocabulary

☐ 5. Enjoys listening to stories and/or poems

☐ 6. Likes to write stories and/or poems

☐ 7. Communicates with others
   in a highly verbal way

☐ 8. Appreciates rhymes, puns, and/or
   nonsense words

☐ 9. Has a good memory for words,
   stories, details

☐ 10. Other linguistic strengths:

   _____

   _____

Logical-Mathematical Intelligence
(Number Smart)

☐ 1. Asks a lot of questions about how
   things work

☐ 2. Has a good sense of cause and effect

☐ 3. Finds math games interesting

☐ 4. Can see and repeat patterns easily

☐ 5. Enjoys working puzzles
   and brain teasers

☐ 6. Understands computer programming

☐ 7. Is a logical thinker

☐ 8. Can estimate things involving numbers
   with relative ease

☐ 9. Can work math concepts in head

☐ 10. Other logical-mathematical strengths:

   _____

   _____

Visual-Spatial Intelligence (Picture Smart)

☐ 1. Reports clear, visual images (or dreams)

☐ 2. Can envision objects from more than
   one perspective

☐ 3. Daydreams more than peers

☐ 4. Likes to draw and/or create art projects

☐ 5. Has a good eye for detail and color

☐ 6. Is good at spatial games like chess and Tetris

☐ 7. Likes movies, slides, or other visual presentations

☐ 8. Can move between 2-dimensional and
   3-dimensional representations with ease

☐ 9. Can read and/or create maps

☐ 10. Other visual-spatial strengths:

   _____

   _____

Bodily-Kinesthetic Intelligence (Body Smart)

☐ 1. Is very coordinated

☐ 2. Exceptionally mobile: moves, twitches,
   fidgets, taps when seated for long

☐ 3. Enjoys working with clay, finger-paint,
   other tactile media

☐ 4. Can mimic others' gestures, posture,
   and movements

☐ 5. Must touch anything new or interesting

☐ 6. Loves to take things apart and
   put them back together

☐ 7. Uses dramatic body movements
   for self-expression

☐ 8. Enjoys running, hopping, climbing, wrestling,
   similar activities

☐ 9. Exhibits fine-motor control (crafts, painting, etc.)

☐ 10. Other bodily-kinesthetic strengths:

   _____

   _____

Adapted by Debbie Silver from Multiple Intelligences in the Classroom by Thomas Armstrong (1994)

Checklist for Assessing "How" Students Are Smart
(continued)

Name of Student: _____

Musical Intelligence (Music Smart)

☐ 1. Can detect music that is off-key, off-beat, or disturbing in some way

☐ 2. Remembers melodies of songs

☐ 3. Taps rhythmically as he/she works or plays

☐ 4. Sensitive to environmental noise (rain on the windows, etc.)

☐ 5. Plays a musical instrument and/or sings in a choir

☐ 6. Has a good singing voice

☐ 7. Responds favorably when music is played

☐ 8. Sings songs that he/she has learned

☐ 9. Unconsciously hums much of the time

☐ 10. Other musical strengths:

_____

_____

Intrapersonal Awareness Intelligence (Self-Smart)

☐ 1. Displays a sense of strong will

☐ 2. Enjoys playing or working alone

☐ 3. Has high self-esteem

☐ 4. Has a good sense of self-direction

☐ 5. Does not mind being different from others

☐ 6. Has a realistic view of his or her strengths and/or weaknesses

☐ 7. Is able to deal effectively with successes and failures

☐ 8. Has an interest or talent not readily shared with others

☐ 9. Seems to "march to the beat of a different drummer"

☐ 10. Other intrapersonal awareness strengths:

_____

_____

Interpersonal Communications Intelligence (People Smart)

☐ 1. Establishes meaningful peer relationships

☐ 2. Seems to be a natural leader

☐ 3. Empathizes with others

☐ 4. Likes to play with others

☐ 5. Shows good teamwork skills

☐ 6. Others seek this student's company

☐ 7. Has two or more close friends

☐ 8. Frequently acts as a mediator and/or peace maker

☐ 9. Enjoys teaching others

☐ 10. Other interpersonal communication strengths:

_____

_____

Naturalistic Intelligence (Nature Smart)

☐ 1. Likes to identify & classify living & nonliving things in nature

☐ 2. Cares for pets or animals

☐ 3. Understands repeating patterns in nature and the universe

☐ 4. Seems more "in tune with nature" than peers

☐ 5. Would rather be outside than inside

☐ 6. Has a demonstrated appreciation for a part of the natural world (e.g., dinosaurs, clouds, rocks, etc.)

☐ 7. Likes to garden and/or appreciates plants

☐ 8. Understands and appreciates the environment

☐ 9. Loves to collect things from nature

☐ 10. Other naturalistic strengths:

_____

_____

Adapted by Debbie Silver from _Multiple Intelligences in the Classroom_ by Thomas Armstrong (1994)

Practice Examples:

1. Your primary students are working on beginning consonant blends. Your class has two students who are reading and writing at a fourth-grade level, an ESL student who is struggling just to speak the language, a hearing-impaired child, and three students who have non-medicated ADHD. Design sample instruction, assignments, and assessments that would give all your students a reasonable chance at success while making progress toward your goals.

2. You want to use multiple intelligences to teach and assess fifth-grade students about U.S. state capitals. Design sample instruction, assignments, and assessments that are grounded in different strength areas. (You do not have to use every intelligence for every phase of the process, but each one should be utilized at least once in the unit.)

3. Your state standards dictate that high school chemistry students have a working knowledge of the Periodic Time Table. Some of your students are highly ordered and sequential; they are good at memorizing the elements and their properties. Another group of students seems bored by the monotony of memorizing the elements and their subatomic particles. Still other students are not able even to pronounce the names of the elements, much less understand their subatomic composition and their purpose. Design sample instruction, assignments, and possible alternative assessments that would help every student meet the standard you are addressing.

It Wasn't My Fault

The Story Behind the Song

We all make excuses. We all deny we did things and put the blame on others. "It Wasn't My Fault" pushes this premise to the extreme and allows us to laugh as we gain perspective. I wrote this song with my brother Mark. Mark is a professional musician, songwriter, and recording artist. He wrote the Dixie Chicks' first #1 hit "There's Your Trouble" and the amazing #1 rock song "Blue on Black." (It wasn't my fault he got all the talent . . . Mom and Dad loved him more . . . he knows the hot singers . . .)

–Monte

Staff Development Ideas by Kathy Hunt-Ullock

The Focus

To remind teachers that a teacher's job is not only to deliver content, to vary their instructional strategies, to differentiate their instruction, and to raise test scores, but also to truly understand the needs and characteristics of the age group that they are teaching. It is vital that we help members of our education community—both students and teachers—evaluate their circumstances, choose their actions, and make conscious decisions based on the recognized consequences.

The Song

How many students do you know that are swept along with the crowd, doing what everybody else is doing, and failing to think for themselves? The humorous lyrics in "It Wasn't My Fault" remind educators that not only are *students* victims of the *"It wasn't my fault!"* mentality, but *educators* too must also take responsibility for their behaviors and decisions.

How many times have you chosen a teaching strategy because it was the easiest way or the most time-effective approach without evaluating the circumstances, studying the options, and making a conscious decision? Here is an opportunity to address the topic of considering consequences, thinking about making informed decisions, and realizing that "It Wasn't My Fault" applies to teachers as well as students.

The Hook

Ask each person to take a few minutes to think about a time when they reprimanded a student and the answer back to them was, "It wasn't my fault!"

It Wasn't My Fault

CHORUS: It wasn't my fault. I'm not the one to blame.
I've got a real good excuse for being in the wrong place
At the wrong time.
Hangin' with a bad crowd,
Just a little too loud.
When we got caught, Hey it wasn't my fault.

Now everybody's pickin' on me,
Everybody's on my case.
Too many people pointing their fingers getting in my face.
Without just cause or reason to believe.
I'm just a fall guy, why can't they see?

CHORUS: It wasn't my fault. I'm not the one to blame.
I've got a real good excuse for being in the wrong place
At the wrong time.
Hangin' with a bad crowd,
Just a little too loud.
When we got caught, Hey it wasn't my fault.

You call that evidence?
You can't trust DNA
And those photographs?
That could be anybody's face.
If you really must know, I've got an evil twin.
He shares my name, and even my fingerprints.

CHORUS: It wasn't my fault. I'm not the one to blame.
I've got a real good excuse for being in the wrong place
At the wrong time.
Hangin' with a bad crowd,
Just a little too loud.
When we got caught, Hey it wasn't my fault.

– Monte and Mark Selby
©2002 Blue Otis Music/
Songs of Moraine, BMI/
Street Singer Music, BMI

Activities for a Large Group

Share Funny Stories

Purpose:

To initiate a conversation about the responsibility of making thoughtful and educated decisions whether you are a student or an educator

Materials:

Step-by-step:

1. After hearing the song, have participants sit at tables in groups of four or five. Number each table.

2. In the table groups have each person tell a funny story about a time when they reprimanded a student or a group of students and the student's reply was, "It wasn't my fault."

3. Ask participants to switch gears and think about the last time they said, "It wasn't my fault." What was the reason for their response? Was the reason similar to the reason for the student's response?

4. Spend a few minutes brainstorming possible ways to reduce the number of "not my fault" responses.

Learn from Your Experience

Purpose:

- To help teachers identify ways to help students avoid "falling into holes" as they make decisions

- To help a staff eliminate problems that recur and keep them from progressing

Materials:

- Copies of *Autobiography in Five Short Chapters* by Portia Nelson. Available online at www.uscis.gov/graphics/services/asylum/poem.htm

- Copies of *Climbing to School* (page 83)

Step-by-step:

1. Read the poem by Portia Nelson to the entire group.

2. Hand out to each person a copy of the poem and the comic strip *Climbing to School*.

3. Place the audience into groups of four or five and number each table.

4. Have each group answer the following three questions:

   a) How are the poem and the comic strip related to the job of a teacher?

   b) What are some of the *holes* or *hills* that your students encounter on a regular basis? What are some of the *holes* or *hills* that you encounter on a regular basis?

   c) How can you, as a teacher, help students walk around those holes or hills and eventually walk down a different street or take off their skates? How can you walk around your own holes or hills and locate a better path?

5. Within the next two weeks, visit a grade level, team, or department meeting. Take extra copies of Portia Nelson's poem to each meeting. Ask the group to list specific ways that their group has helped kids out of holes, and actions they have taken to help kids walk around hills. Ask if there are places you as an administrator or facilitator can help to eliminate holes or hills for staff and students.

Activity for a Small Group

Who Has the Power?

Purpose:

- To help teachers feel that they can make informed decisions instead of being powerless bystanders
- To recognize the importance of collaborative, inquiry-based learning

Materials:

- Large piece of newsprint
- Colored markers and crayons

Step-by-step:

1. Ask members of the group to respond to these questions:
   Who determines what will be taught in your classroom?
   Who determines how it will be taught?

2. When the group has come to a consensus, compare the results to this statement by Catherine Twomey Fosnot:

   Children sit for 12 years in classrooms where the implicit goal is to listen to the teacher and memorize the information in order to regurgitate it on a test. Little or no attention is paid to the learning process.

3. Challenge the group to brainstorm ways in which students and teachers can both be active participants in the learning/teaching model. Learners who perceive themselves in control of the process are less likely to say, "It wasn't my fault."

> ## Activity for Individuals

Taking Responsibility

Purpose:

To encourage teachers to consider new approaches to instruction, including inquiry-based student-centered learning

Materials:

- Journal or computer
- Pen and pencil or computer paper

Step-by-step:

Respond to this statement:

Rather than being powerless and dependent on the teacher, students need to be empowered to think and to learn for themselves. Learning needs to be thought of as something a learner does, not something that is done to a learner.
— Fosnot

Do you agree? What implications does this statement have for classroom instruction? for curriculum development? for assessment?

Reproduce this page at 120% for 8½ x 11 size. Use it with the activity on page 80.

Climbing to School

Fly on the Wall

The Story Behind the Song

Have you ever called a meeting with parents to discuss a kid who's acting out, only to have the parents explain that they are having problems and getting a divorce, but their children don't know about it yet? Obviously the child knew more than the parents thought. I remember hearing the phrase, "If you're going to whisper it in the lounge, you might as well use the school loudspeaker." A word or a look has the power to instill hopelessness or hope. I suggest that you look at the song in two ways: First, watch where and what you say and second, imagine the power of whispering each morning, *"I know you can do it, I know you can do it . . ."*.

–Monte

Staff Development Ideas by Debbie Silver and Monte Selby

The Focus

To raise adult awareness of how expectations (both stated and unstated) can impact student motivation, development, and achievement.

The Song

The song "Fly on the Wall," although deceptively simple, contains a powerful message about teacher expectations and student achievement. The activities provided challenge all staff members to:

- First, make sure each student knows that an adult cares about his/her success at school (connectedness);
- Second, reflect upon current expectations and practices at school; and
- Third, offer research and resources to large groups, small groups, and individuals.

The Activities

The first large group activity engages participants in a process to quickly identify the "connected" students at school. In the second activity, volunteers are asked to role-play a student who is given persistent negative responses from the adults in her/his life. Participants are also asked to list and consider teacher behaviors that communicate positive expectations to students.

In the small group sessions, participants are asked to reflect on corollaries drawn from Rosenthal's research on *self-fulfilling prophecy*. They recall anecdotes from their personal histories that validate the corollaries. In the second small group activity, adults select one of the novel approaches provided to "reconnect" students identified in the large group activity.

For the individual follow-up activities, participants can respond to quotes about education in their personal journals. A second activity guides students in the creation of simple "highlight" videos intended to support teacher and student expectations.

The Hook

Imagine that one of your students (perhaps one that is a particular challenge) is "a fly on the wall" and can see and hear all that you say . . .

Fly on the Wall

There's a fly on the wall
And little pictures with ears
Using magic recorders
For every word they hear
It might be under the breath
Or whispered from the start
But everything we say about kids—
Soon they'll know by heart

CHORUS: Might as well write it on the lockers
Write it on the wall
Write it on the forehead of a kid for all to see—
Self-fulfilling prophecy
I don't know how it happens
An unsolved mystery
But all kids learn what adults believe
They can or could or can't or should or will

Now some kids are slow to comprehend
No matter how many times we explain
And it's all we can do not to whine and complain
But every new idea or effort
Strategy, plan, or gimmick
Is a message read loud and clear—
It gives hope when we're optimistic

CHORUS: Sort of like we write it on the lockers
Write it on the wall
Write it on the forehead of a kid for all to see—
Self-fulfilling prophecy
And I don't know how it happens
An unsolved mystery
But all kids learn what adults believe
They can or could or can't or should or will
I don't know how it happens
Probably never will
How a word or look
Has the power to instill
They can or should or can't or could or will

– Monte Selby
©2004 Street Singer Music, BMI

 **Fly on the Wall**

Identifying Connected Students

Purpose:

- To quickly identify students who have (or lack) a healthy connection with adults at school
- To consider the implications of having more students connect with adults at school

Materials:

- List of all students, displayed in large type
- Adhesive colored "dots"

Step-by-step:

Preparation: The names of all students attending school should be displayed around the perimeter of the room. The names should be easy to read in a large, simple font. Staff members (including teachers, paraprofessionals, custodians, secretaries, bus drivers, etc.) will need space to move about the room and access the lists. All adults should be provided plenty of "dots" (the small colorful adhesive round dots used to price items at garage sales). Dots can be purchased in the office supply section of many stores.

1. The facilitator asks participants to stick a dot next to the names of students with whom they are positively connected. Guide the process with a statement like: "Consider students who have personally shared a story with you, or with whom you have a positive shared experience. Do not "dot" students that you can simply identify by name or appearance."

2. Participants then move throughout the room to place dots next to students with whom they have a "connection." The amount of time required will obviously be determined by the number of students listed.

3. As participants return to their seats, ask them to take note of students with few or zero dots.

4. Please take time to mention that students identified by the activity should not be discussed publicly! The purpose is to highlight possible needs and consider follow-up options.

5. Reflection questions to be considered:

   a) Do we have any reason to believe that students who are better connected with adults at school are more likely to succeed?

   b) Do those adults necessarily have to be teachers?

   c) As a group, are we interested in exploring strategies to better connect with students who have few or zero dots?

   d) At a future meeting, would you like to explore the small group activity provided (below) with simple strategies to help "connect" these students?

   e) If we don't want to explore a formal process or strategy, everyone is welcome to simply take note of a student who seems to lack adult connections and engage that student on a weekly basis.

How Teachers Communicate Expectations

Purpose:

- To help teachers understand the principles of self-fulfilling prophecy theory
- To create an awareness of how teacher behavior (both overt and covert) affects student achievement

Materials:

- Poster Paper
- Markers
- A sign labeled "IALAC"

Step-by-step:

1. Give teachers a brief background of the SFP Theory.

2. Ask volunteers to demonstrate the "IALAC" activity. One volunteer takes on the role of a student in your school. She or he holds a sign that has these large letters—I A L A C. The leader explains that the letters stand for the idea, "I Am Lovable And Capable." The leader asks the student to demonstrate when those feelings are diminished by ripping off a piece of the sign when he or she hears or feels something that communicates low expectations. (Just rip off a piece of paper and let it fall to the floor.)

   The remaining volunteers are asked to be adults in the *student's* typical day.

Roles can differ, but you might want to have a parent, a bus driver, an administrator, and a few teachers. Each of those people says or does something to the *student* that conveys a negative expectation about her/him.

The skit continues until there is nothing left of the sign.

The leader then asks the group to consider how the *student* is now feeling with all the paper strewn around her/his feet.

Discuss how student learning can be impacted by such interactions with the adults at school.

3. The leader asks participants (in whole group or in small groups) to list on their poster paper some possible ways teachers can communicate expectations in ways other than words. Have group members present their lists. Participants may vary their responses, but some possible answers to expect are:

   - Seating low expectation students far from the teacher and/or seating them in a group.
   - Paying less attention to lows in academic situations (smiling less often, maintaining less eye contact, etc.)
   - Calling on lows less often to answer questions or make a public demonstration.
   - Waiting less time for lows to answer a question.
   - Not staying with lows in failure situations (i.e., providing fewer prompts, asking fewer follow-up questions).
   - Criticizing lows more frequently than highs for incorrect responses,
   - Praising lows less frequently than highs after successful responses.
   - Praising highs more frequently than lows for marginal or inadequate responses.
   - Providing lows with less accurate and less detailed feedback than highs.
   - Failing to provide lows with feedback about their responses as often as highs.

   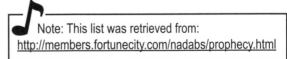
   Note: This list was retrieved from: http://members.fortunecity.com/nadabs/prophecy.html

   - Demanding less work and effort from lows than from highs.
   - Interrupting lows more frequently than highs.

4. Ask teachers to consider the statements they have made in the last week directly to students or in their presence. In small groups, ask them to share something they said or did that they would now change if they could.

Activities for a Small Group

Self-Fulfilling Prophecy in the Classroom

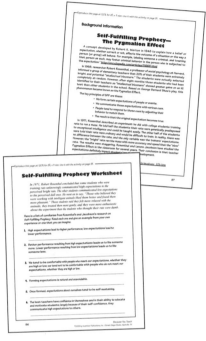

Purpose:

- To help teachers understand the effects of self-fulfilling prophecy in the classroom

- To focus on the positive aspects of self-fulfilling prophecy

Materials:

- Copies of "Self-Fulfilling Prophecy Worksheet" (page 96)

- Poster paper and marking pens

Step-by-step:

1. Give group members a copy of the worksheet.

2. Ask teachers to read each corollary put forth by Robert Rosenthal (1971), and ask them to write an anecdote, real or imagined, representative of each one.

3. Have group members share their examples. Discuss the implications of the stories they present.

4. Ask group members to generate a list of constructive ways teachers can communicate positive expectations to students. Include words, phrases, gestures, and other nonverbal means of communication.

5. Record the group's ideas on poster paper.

6. Have someone type the ideas listed on the poster paper and distribute them to group members as a reminder about self-fulfilling prophecy.

♪ Note: If participants are not familiar with Rosenthal's *Theory of Self-Fulfilling Prophecy*, reproduce the background information on page 97 and review it with them.

Supporting Adult-Student Connectedness

Purpose:

To pursue at least one positive adult connection for each student in school using simple, easy strategies

Materials:

Computer

Step-by-step:

Option 1: Tell me about it!

1. At a meeting with all interested staff, allow adults to choose a student or several students with whom they are likely to have at least weekly contact. Regardless of the adult's position, the purpose is to take a personal interest in the student.

2. Consider using the phrase "tell me about it." This non-judgmental phrase allows the adult to quickly open a conversation on the student's "turf." For instance, "tell me about your ball game last night", "tell me about your skateboard", "tell me about how that iPod works", "tell me about your nose ring", "tell me about how you get your hair to look that way", "tell me about what's for lunch today", "tell me what's good on TV", or "tell me what you think about the war."

Option 2: Help me create a blog!

1. Consider a "blog" site for a class, an advisory group, a team, etc. A blog is simply the popular term for "web log." The adult does not have to be a tech expert! Ask if there is a student willing to help set up the site—the only requirement is access to an online computer. It is important that the adult is the only person with the password. Student postings to the site should be monitored at school!

2. The adult determines what appropriate content to allow students to post, for example favorite activities, music, animals, sports teams, books, etc. Each student is allowed time to post information.

> ♪ Note: A blog is accessed on the Internet, which is exciting to students, but also carries responsibility for the sponsor.

3. The adult takes time to read and remember information about students who lack connections to adults at school. Each time more information is added to the blog, the adult can ask the students more about their interests in music, sports, books, etc.

4. If the identified students have an interest, allow them opportunities to bring the blog "to life" with color and font changes or by adding appropriate images, links, and cartoons. It is not difficult. Students need the opportunity and time, not training! The adult role is taking an interest and providing adequate supervision.

5. This activity helps connect each student to the adult, the other students, and to school. It proclaims "somebody cares about what I think and do!"

Option 3: I heard it through the grapevine.

1. At a meeting with all interested staff, allow adults to identify students with whom they are likely to have at least weekly contact.

2. The adult role is to seek out from teachers, coaches, sponsors, students, or through general observation any bits of information that indicate something the student does well. The adult makes it a point each week to have one positive observation. For instance, "Hey, Bobby, I heard through the grapevine that you have a trombone solo at the concert," or "I heard you can do tricks with your bike, is that true?"

3. All students and adults like knowing that other people are noticing and saying good things about them . . . through the grapevine.

Activities for Individuals

The Power of One

Purpose:

- To help individuals reflect on the power they have with students
- To reiterate the importance of considering self-fulfilling prophecy when planning best practices

 **Fly on the Wall**

Materials:

Personal journals

Step-by-step:

Read the following list of quotations and pick one (or more) that is particularly meaningful. In your personal journal, write the thought you chose and an anecdotal response to the truism. Explain how the quotation fits with self-fulfilling prophecy theory.

A. "If you treat an individual as he is, he will stay as he is, but if you treat him as if he were what he ought to be and could be, he will become what he ought to be and could be."

–Johann Wolfgang Goethe, German writer and philosopher

B. "The people who influence you are the people who believe in you."

–Henry Drummond, British religious leader and writer

C. "Our lives are shaped by those who love us, and those who refuse to love us."

–John Powell, professor of theology

D. "To me education is a leading out of what is already there in a pupil's soul."

–Muriel Spark, British writer

E. "Children are apt to live up to what you believe of them."

–Lady Bird Johnson, former First Lady of the U.S.

F. "Act as if what you do makes a difference. It does."

–William James, American psychologist and philosopher

G. "What we are teaches the child far more than what we say, so we must be what we want our children to become."

–Joseph Chilton Pearce, American lecturer and writer

H. "The secret in education lies in respecting the student."

–Ralph Waldo Emerson, American poet, essayist, lecturer

I. "Don't judge each day by the harvest you reap, but by the seeds you plant."

–Robert Louis Stevenson, Scottish writer

Because You Teach

Teacher Expectation Highlight Film

Purpose:

To make sure expectations are clarified and demonstrated—not assumed

Materials:

Video recording and editing equipment

Step-by-step:

1. Sports teams and dance teams are most often featured in highlight films. A highlight film says "These are the people who do it best, and this is the best of what they do." The question is: "In our school, what behaviors would make the highlight film demonstrating the best of what we do?"

2. The challenge is: "Can we articulate what it is we want—the behaviors we would like to see more students doing more of the time—and allow students to catch examples of that on film?"

3. Can we create a highlight film with:

   • Students who are supporting other students?

   • Students being helpful and polite in the hall?

   • Students demonstrating appropriate (and fun) behavior in the cafeteria?

   • Students who are great fans at ball games?

   • Students who create interesting projects for class?

   • Students who organize their lockers well?

   • Students who play well with others at recess?

   • Or . . . ?

Self-Fulfilling Prophecy Worksheet

In 1971, Robert Rosenthal concluded that some students who were training rats unknowingly communicated high expectations to the perceived bright rats. The other students communicated low expectations to the perceived dull ones. He went on to say, "Those who believed they were working with intelligent animals liked them better and found them more pleasant." Those students said they felt more relaxed with the animals, they treated them more gently, and they were more enthusiastic about the experiment than the students who thought their rats were dumb.

Here is a list of corollaries from Rosenthal's and Jacobson's research on *Self-Fulfilling Prophecy.* Read each one and give an example from your own experience or one that you can imagine.

1. High expectations lead to higher performance; low expectations lead to lower performance.

_____

2. Better performance resulting from high expectations leads us to like someone more. Lower performance resulting from low expectations leads us to like someone less.

_____

3. We tend to be comfortable with people who meet our expectations, whether they are high or low; we tend not to be comfortable with people who do not meet our expectations, whether they are high or low.

_____

4. Forming expectations is natural and unavoidable.

_____

5. Once formed, expectations about ourselves tend to be self-sustaining.

_____

6. The best teachers have confidence in themselves and in their ability to educate and motivate students; largely because of their self-confidence, they communicate high expectations to others.

_____

Because You Teach
©2006 by Incentive Publications, Inc./Street Singer Books, Nashville, TN

Background Information

Self-Fulfilling Prophecy—
The Pygmalion Effect

A concept developed by Robert K. Merton in 1948 to explain how a belief or expectation, whether correct or not, affects the outcome of a situation or the way a person (or group) will behave. For example, labeling someone a criminal, and treating that person as such, may foster criminal behavior in the person who is subjected to the expectation." http://encyclopedia.com/articles/11668.html

In 1968, researcher Robert Rosenthal, a professor of social psychology at Harvard, informed a group of elementary teachers that 20% of their students were extremely bright and potential "intellectual bloomers." The students were actually selected completely at random. However, after eight months those students who had been identified to their teachers as "intellectual bloomers" showed greater gains on an IQ test than other students in the school. Based on George Bernard Shaw's play, this phenomenon became known as the Pygmalion Effect.

The key principles of SFP are these:

- We form certain expectations of people or events.
- We communicate those expectations with various cues.
- People tend to respond to these cues by adjusting their behavior to match them.
- The result is that the original expectation becomes true.

In 1971, Rosenthal described an experiment he did with college students training rats to run a maze. He told half the students their rats were genetically predisposed to exceptional intelligence and could be taught easily. The other half of the students were told their rats were ordinary and would be difficult to train. In reality, there was no difference between the rats, and the only variable was the trainers' expectations. However, the "bright" rats ran the maze with more accuracy and speed than the "slow" rats. The results were staggering. Rosenthal and Lenore Jacobson have studied the Pygmalion Effect in the classroom for several years. Their conclusion is that teacher expectations definitely impact students' intellectual development.

http://westrek.hypermart.net/mangmnt_artcls/motivate_02b.htm

No Excuse

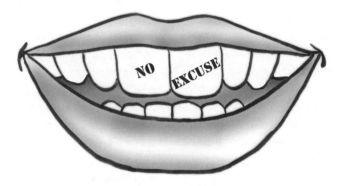

The Story Behind the Song

When I work with students, this is the song they most often request. Why do kids like this song so much? They say that the teacher in the song holds firm to high expectations, but still has a smile. The song is a tribute to teachers who enjoy the whole child—to those who recognize the good and the bad, and who appreciate the growing-up process. Imagine how students would feel if you had "No Excuse" tattooed on your front teeth.

—Monte

Staff Development Ideas by Rick Wormeli

The Focus

As students get older, they learn the art of rationalizing. They talk themselves and others into their own way of thinking. The problem is that they can be so egocentric, they cannot see the shortcomings of their own reasoning:

- "Of course I was late with the work," they reason, "no one gave me a pencil to use."

- "It's excusable that I was late to class," they rationalize, "because I forgot my supplies and had to go back across the school to my locker to get them, and then on the way back here, I was stopped by a friend of mine who needed to borrow my TI-83 for his class, and I had to fish it out of my book bag for him."

When students offer excuses, they are testing the waters:

- What is normal and what is not normal?

- Can I get away with this?

- What will society tolerate as acceptable and part of being human?

They are also trying to explain their behaviors to themselves:

- Who am I, and how did I get into this mess?

- How do I save face in light of this mistake I've made?

Effective teachers consider what is and is not acceptable in terms of student behavior, as well as how to communicate those attributes to students in ways in which students learn them. Simply admonishing students for not choosing correct behaviors isn't teaching.

Teachers should also remember that they are not teaching adults with adult-level competencies. Students up through the junior year of high school are focused on how to live this one week of their lives. They are focused on the here and now; telling them that eight years from now they will have to be on time for meetings has no currency.

In addition, as non-adults, students are learning to behave in a consistently mature manner, but they aren't there yet. They can intellectualize that they should do something like study for a test or clean up in one class so they are not late for the next one, but they are tired and have low impulsivity control, and they decide to listen to one more song on a classmate's iPod. They require repeated learning experiences with self-discipline and making mature responses, not one lesson at the beginning of the year and the rest of the year an assumption that they've mastered these skills. Yes, we hold students accountable for poor decisions, but we choose to be instructive, not punitive in our responses, and we don't take it personally or declare the end of civilization when they digress.

The Song

Monte's song recognizes the importance of consistency in dealing with excuses while at the same time acknowledging the creativity shown by the excuse-makers.

The Hook

Think about the best excuses you have heard and imagine what your *excuse journal* would look like.

No Excuse

My teacher loves excuses, they only make her laugh
She writes them in her notebook, then converts to charts and graphs
Statistical analysis is the game she's learned to play
Just to see who is most likely to use which excuse which day
I think she's kind of twisted and craves to give abuse,
So take advice from victims—there ain't no good excuse.

Some kids are real creative, can make up lies with style
But every explanation, it only fuels her fire
She adores elaborate schemes that justify the cause
Of dark and evil plotters who'd lose homework to a dog
She shines her wicked smile, tattoo on her front tooth
You'll see it while you're crying, it just reads, "no excuse."

Well, they say that she'll be rich, have millions in the bank
She plans to write a book, for kids in every grade
She'll have one category for every single need
With mathematical probabilities of what teachers will believe
An underground bestseller when she retires and turns it loose
No kid will be defenseless from the queens
    (and kings and bad dreams) of, "no excuse."

I got no excuse . . .

– Monte Selby

Activity for a Large Group

"Late Again—What's Your Excuse?"

Purpose:

> To sensitize faculty members to the nature of human excuses and how best to respond to them

Materials:

- A large meeting room and seat for everyone
- A pretend (or real) agenda for a faculty meeting

Step-by-step:

1. Ask a few members of the faculty to be part of a secret, role-playing simulation for the next faculty meeting. Have them arrive a few minutes late, after you've started the meeting.

2. As the latecomers enter, stop what you're doing and comment on how you've noticed that some staff members are not being very courteous to others in that they show up late to meetings. Explain that you know their lives are busy, but that it would really help the meeting and show professional respect for colleagues if everyone could arrange their lives so they could be here on time.

3. Ask these late arriving teachers to explain why they were late. Make sure each one replies with a different reason—some acceptable and some not. Examples of excuses might include:

   - "The photocopier broke down mid-copying and I didn't want to leave the mess for someone else to handle."

   - "I had a parent phone call and the parent was very distraught. I had to get her calmed down before hanging up."

   - "The traffic was really heavy today, and I was stuck behind a school bus making stops almost all the way here."

   - "The activity I did today with students was unusually messy, and I needed to clear it up a bit before the custodial staff came in to clean."

- "I was online and lost track of the time."

- "I thought the meeting actually started 15 minutes later, and I was early."

- "I was on bus duty and bus 4 was 10 minutes late."

- "I didn't know there was a meeting today until I passed by and saw everyone in here."

- "I had to get this grant proposal paperwork over to the administration office before 2:00 today."

4. Try to stay in character and keep a straight face as teachers give you their excuses, then turn to the group and ask, "Are these acceptable excuses?"

5. Once you've brainstormed a bit, ask the faculty to identify acceptable reasons for being late to a faculty meeting. This can be done orally. Once listed, ask them to list unacceptable reasons for being late to a faculty meeting. Again, this can be done orally.

6. At this point, "break character" if you haven't already and reveal the simulation nature of this experience, explaining that the tardiness of the teachers, as well as your response to them, was a setup. This will encourage the rest of the faculty to speak freely in the next step.

7. Now, ask the faculty what response should be made to those who arc late to faculty meetings. At some point, ask whether or not a different response should be made to those who are frequently late versus those who are rarely late but are late this one time.

8. Finally, ask teachers how this scenario is the same and different when it comes to listening to students' excuses for poor decisions, such as being late to class, late with work, coming to class without requested supplies, or when not being prepared for class. What should be remembered when working with students who chronically come up with excuses, and what should be remembered when working with students who are only occasionally lax in their responsibilities?

9. A spin-off question at this point might be to ask whether or not all teachers must have the same policies regarding these issues. There are arguments for and against such attempts at consistency.

Activity for a Small Group

The Dog Ate My Homework

Purpose:

- To recognize that educators have different tolerance levels for excuses
- To develop a repertoire of positive responses to excuses

Materials:

Paper and marking pens

Step-by-step:

1. Place teachers in small groups, preferably by grade level (different grade levels have different issues).

2. Ask each group to brainstorm as many excuses as they can that students have used for not having work completed, not having supplies, for talking when they weren't supposed to, or for being late to class.

3. Now ask them to classify which one excuses are legitimate. In many of these groups, teachers will discover that they have different levels of tolerance from one another, and they have different interpretations of student behaviors.

4. Once done, ask groups to respond to the following questions:

   - Why do students make excuses for their poor choices and/or behaviors?

   - What does a highly accomplished teacher do when he or she hears a student's excuse?

   - What kind of classroom atmosphere is ripe for students' excuse-making, and what kind of atmosphere would lower the amount of excuses students felt they could give? If comfortable, ask, "Which kind of classroom do you have?"

   - How can we get students to limit or even eliminate their automatic default response of making excuses when they have performed or behaved poorly? List at least five learning experiences a teacher at this grade level could provide that would enable students to take responsibility for their actions. Collect these from each group and compile a list of all of them for the faculty to reference throughout the year.

   - How should we respond differently to students who are chronically late or misbehaving versus those who are only occasionally late or misbehaving, and is it okay to give different responses to different students? Why or why not?

- How do we keep our attitudes toward students positive even when they make these mistakes repeatedly?
- How can we "read" a student to tell whether or not he or she is telling the truth?

Activity for Individuals

Late-Work Policies

Purpose:

To develop a policy for accepting late work

Materials:

"Late Work: A Constructive Response" (pages 106–109)

Step-by-step:

1. Read the article "Late Work: A Constructive Response."

2. Reflect on the following questions:
   - With what did you agree?
   - With what did you disagree?
   - What are your late-work policies?
   - Are your responses to late work meant to punish students, teach students, or both?
   - Identify the elements of your late-work policies that demonstrate your expertise in what is developmentally appropriate for the students you teach.
   - What evidence do you have that your late-work policies are effective in teaching students how to grow in maturity so as not to be late with their work?
   - Are there other late-work policies you'd be interested in exploring with your students? If so, identify them.
   - Besides placing marks in a grade book, how do we best teach students in your grade level to be self-disciplined and to take responsibility for themselves?

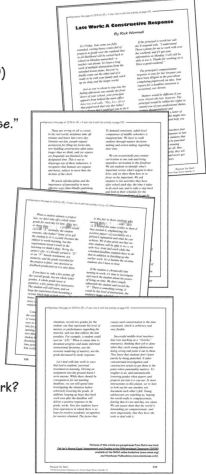

Late Work: A Constructive Response

By Rick Wormeli

It's Friday. Your arms are fully extended, carting heavy crates full of projects to grade over the weekend that in all likelihood will be carted back to school on Monday untouched—a teacher can dream. It's been a long week of multiple distractions from the intended lesson plans, but you've finally come out the other end of it ready to be with your family and catch up on sleep and the larger world.

Just as you're about to step into the fading afternoon sun outside the front doors of your school, your principal appears from behind the main office doorway and calls, "Hey, how about that paperwork that was due today? Any chance that I could get you to do it before you leave? It should only take 20 minutes or so."

You grind to a halt, heart sinking, and turn to face your administrator. "Oh, wow," you begin. "I'm really sorry I didn't finish that. We had the field trip this week, and testing meetings the last couple of afternoons. I completely forgot, but I really need to get home to my family. Is there any way I can work on it over the weekend and get it to you first thing Monday morning?"

If the principal is worth her salt she'll respond with, "I understand. There's plenty for me to work with over the weekend, and if I get your information on Monday, I will still be able to use it. Thanks for working on it. Have a good weekend."

The principal's compassionate response is easy for her because you have been diligent in the past about completing paperwork on time. Your request for a deadline extension is occasional, not chronic.

Matters would be different if you were chronically late, however. The principal would be within her rights to remind you of your professional duties, express disappointment and frustration, and even put a letter of reprimand in your file. She might also take time to investigate and help you reprioritize your time.

Many middle school teachers fear that a compassionate response to late student work will teach students that it's okay for them not to be punctual or heed deadlines. The ensuing anarchy would engulf us all, they fear, and in the real world, they tell their students, you would never get away with such behaviors.

These are wrong on all accounts. In the real world, airplanes take off minutes and hours late every day. Dentists run late, people request permission for filing tax forms late, new building construction often takes longer than we think, and car repairs are frequently not finished by the designated time. This is not to disparage any of these industries; it recognizes that humans are organic and messy, subject to more than the dictates of the clock.

We teach self-discipline and the importance of punctuality in more effective ways than blindly punishing students. For instance, we share stories of individuals who were and were not on time with their tasks and the consequences in each case. We show students the high achievement that can be reached by on-time completions. We provide students with individual feedback regarding their punctuality, we emphasize formative assessment and feedback over summative versions so students stay on course, and we structure our lessons so students want to keep up with work in order to fully participate in compelling experiences and to not be overwhelmed by playing catch-up with too many tasks at one time.

We also must realize that we are not teaching full-grown adults with adult-level competencies. We are teaching young adolescents who are learning those competencies for the first time.

To demand consistent, adult-level competence of middle schoolers is inappropriate. We have to walk students through mature decision-making and action-taking regarding their time.

We can occasionally put content curriculum to one side and bring unspoken curriculum to the forefront: We ask students to identify what's important versus what's urgent in their lives, and we show them how to re-focus on the important. We ask students to list activities they have after school each day, the time it takes to do each one, and to take a step back and look at their schedule for the whole week to see if any of it can be rearranged or reprioritized.

We help students set up Calendars of Completion with which we break down large tasks into daily smaller tasks. We help them record what they need to do on Thursday before a big project is due on Friday, then what they need to do on Wednesday so they can do those tasks on Thursday, then what they should do on Tuesday so they can do the tasks on Wednesday so they can do the tasks on Thursday so they can turn in the project on Friday. We work backwards with students until the present day. The time spent doing this is invaluable to middle school students—where and when else might they learn this? There are even some of us adults who could benefit from someone guiding our time management.

When a student submits a project late, we don't take off a whole letter grade for each day it's late. After two or three days, even if the project would earn an "A" normally, the student reasons, why bother? Some of us tell the student to do it anyway because the subject is worth learning, but this requirement doesn't result in the learning we think it does. Doing the project after it's already earned a "D" or an "F" breeds resentment, not maturity, and the grade recorded for the project is false—any decision or feedback predicated on it is also false.

If you have to, take a few points off the overall grade, but not whole letter grades. A whole grade lower is punitive, a few points off is instructive. The student will still learn, and we keep the experience from becoming a vicious black hole to both parties. Even better, the student learns and the grade stays close to being an accurate rendering of mastery.

Consider: If the student is late with the work only occasionally (i.e., once or twice a grading period), then it's easy to be merciful. Let him turn it in late for full credit. Just as in the opening example, teachers and others turn things in late all the time. The student has earned our goodwill and flexibility with weeks or months of on-time performance, so we can extend him civility.

Is this fair to those students who turned their work in on time? Sure. We'd extend the same civility to them if they needed it, emphasizing the positive impact of punctuality on a person's reputation and what he can achieve. We'd also point out that on-time students will be able to move on with their lives and work while the extended-deadline students have to do that in addition to finishing up the earlier work. It's a burden the on-time students don't have to bear.

If the student is chronically late turning in work, it's time to investigate and teach the student about the power of being on time. We don't simply admonish the student and record the "F." There is something wrong. It could be the level of instruction, the student's home schedule, an emotional issue, lack of resources, cultural insensitivity, miscommunication, auditory processing issues, or something else. We help students advocate for themselves, not just hold them accountable. Student accountability without purpose is one reason why students drop out and schools fail.

Because your colleagues may lower grades by a full letter grade and you want to keep the peace, you may have to do it as well. The problem, of course, is that this new grade is tainted and is no longer useful. In these situations, record two grades for the student: one that represents his level of mastery or performance regarding the material, and one that reflects the late penalties. For example, a student could earn an "A/D." When it comes time to document progress and make informed instructional decisions, use the accurate rendering of mastery, not the grade decreased by tardy response.

Let's deal with late work in ways that lead to students' personal investment in learning. Driving an assignment into the ground doesn't serve anyone. While there should be consequences for not meeting deadlines, we can still spend time investigating the situation before arbitrarily lowering the grade. In addition, keeping up hope that hard work even after the deadline will deliver a positive response in the grade, works. Very few students learn from experiences in which there is no hope for positive academic recognition for mastery obtained. The factor that

causes such consternation is the time constraint, which is arbitrary and very fixable.

Successful middle-level teachers don't see teaching as a "Gotcha" enterprise, thinking their job is done when they catch young adolescents doing wrong and point it out to them. They know that students don't learn purely by being punished. It takes concentrated investigation and constructive action to get them to the point where punctuality matters. It's tougher to do, and automatically lowering grades when papers and projects are late is a cop-out. In most interactions on this planet, we're here to look out for one another, not document each other's fall. Young adolescents are watching us, hoping the world really is compassionate, fearing that it's not and they are alone. We can assure them that the world is demanding yet compassionate, and more importantly, that they have the tools to deal with it.

Portions of this article are paraphrased from Rick's new book
<u>Fair Isn't Always Equal: Assessment and Grading in the Differentiated Classroom (2006)</u>
available at the NMSA online bookstore (www.nmsa.org)
and Stenhouse Publications (www.stenhouse.com).

Who's Got That Vision?

The Story Behind the Song

I was driving from home in Kansas to Nebraska. I was on my way to work with some fourth-graders. As I prepared my presentation in my head, I carried on a conversation with the imagined students. My head was filled with the great ideas that come from kids. The song "Who's Got That Vision?" wrote itself during that drive.

—Monte

Staff Development Ideas by Debbie Silver

The Focus

To help participants focus on the importance of individual excellence in the classroom and the significance of teachers as leaders.

The Song

Monte's song, "Who's Got That Vision?" can be interpreted to mean that teachers should be advocates for every student because we never know where genius may lie. Or it can be interpreted that teachers should seek the genius within themselves and use that vision to impact education.

The Activities

Select whichever activities work best for your group size and modify them to suit your specific needs. All activities are designed to help teachers reacquaint themselves with their personal power and influence. Both large group activities focus on teacher conviction and courage. The first uses participants' recollections of great teachers to reflect on their own personal vision of teaching. The second asks teachers to work in groups to determine ways they can become more effective teacher leaders.

> ♪ Note: In this particular experience, the large group, small group, and individual activities can be interchanged with a few modifications.

The small group activities are designed to be introspective experiences. While they could also be used as general group activities, their personal nature may lend them better to small, intimate groups. Care should be taken not to ask participants to be more candid than they choose to be; these activities call for mutual trust among group members. If groups have not yet established mutual trust and respect, these activities may be modified to use as individual experiences.

The individual activities involve journal writing and creating a personal belief poster. Sharing their thoughts about these solitary endeavors can be enlightening and instructive for teachers in a group setting.

The Hook

What is your vision for the school year, the upcoming month, this week, your second period class?

Who's Got That Vision?

A young boy carves on the walls of the cave
A few birds and a squirrel
He paints his buddies with their bows and arrows
And his favorite cave girl
And no one can comprehend why he does it
There are better things he should do
But ain't it amazing ten thousand years later
He's left us some pretty good clues

    CHORUS: Now who gets remembered?
                Who really makes that change
                That makes all the difference at some future date?
                Sometimes we're just lucky
                Out on our own little mission
                But you never know for sure
                Who's got that vision

There's a tribe on the move
Got a heavy load
Old woman stops to rest
She draws in the dirt, tells the men to come look
"Here's an idea you should test"
Well the men turn away with a frown and they mutter
"This old woman don't know what's real"
While a young girl watches, puts the thought in her head
And someday she'll make the first wheel

    Repeat CHORUS.

There's a kid in class, a kid in the park
A kid this morning, a kid after dark
A kid that looks funny, a kid that acts mean
That can't sit still, a kid that daydreams
A kid that keeps trying to get our attention
With just one more thing to say
Hey, we never know till we look and listen
That kid found a better way?

                        – Monte Selby
                ©1999 Street Singer Music, BMI

> **Activities for a Large Group**

The Greatest Teacher

Purpose:

- To help participants focus on the importance of having the "courage of one's convictions"
- To encourage teachers to "go outside their comfort zones" to advocate for students

> ♪ Note: This activity should be done BEFORE the song is presented.

Materials:

- Preassigned note cards (for participants to select and list five great teachers)
- Posters
- Marking pens

Step-by-step:

1. Before the meeting, let all participants know they should bring with them a list of the five greatest teachers they can think of (alive or dead, real or fictitious, known personally or not). Tell them they should be prepared to defend their choices.

2. Assign participants into groups of five to seven members each. Be sure that the selection is random, and do not allow participants to choose their own groups.

3. Tell participants that the youngest person (you may use some other arbitrary trait) in each group will serve as the leader. Leaders are to poll group members for their choices of greatest teachers.

4. After a discussion of each member's personal selections, group members should reach consensus on their group's "Top Five."

5. Groups then make a poster with their "Top Five" list. They should fill the white space on the poster with words or phrases describing what makes (or made) these teachers great.

6. Inform the groups that one of them will be presenting their conclusions to the whole group, and you will let them know later who has been selected.

7. After they have had a chance to get their ideas together, use another arbitrary method for your reporter selection (person who has the longest legs, person who

lives the closest to the school, person who has the most college hours, etc.).

8. Ask that person to report her/his group's findings to the rest of the audience.

9. After each group reporter has presented, ask the participants if they see any similarities among the words and phrases that were written about great teachers. Point out words such as *courageous, independent thinker, believed in her/his cause, worked for the greater good, was a visionary, leader,* etc.

10. Give participants a copy of the lyrics for the Monte Selby song "Who's Got That Vision?", and play the song for them. Ask participants how the song applies to teaching. Point out that every teacher has some kind of vision about his or her influence. Ask teachers to reflect on their own personal mission in teaching.

11. Discuss the importance of teacher leadership on behalf of individual students, as well as for the field of education.

12. *(Optional)* Invite audience members to cite instances where their prior teachers or people present in the room acted as a leader for a student, a cause, or a vision.

Teachers as Leaders

Purpose:
- To help teachers focus on their roles as leaders
- To emphasize the importance of teacher leaders
- To determine ways teachers can act as leaders

Materials:
- Giant Post-it™ chart paper to make seven posters
- A pad of small Post-it™ notes for each participant
- Pens or markers

Step-by-step:

1. Prepare the seven posters by printing one of the following at the top of each of the posters:

   a) Teachers can be leaders in the classroom by . . .

   b) Teachers can be leaders in the school by . . .

   c) Teachers can be leaders in the district by . . .

   d) Teachers can be leaders in the state by . . .

e) Teachers can be leaders in the region by . . .

f) Teachers can be leaders in the nation by . . .

g) Teachers can be leaders in the world by . . .

Post the posters around the meeting room.

2. As participants enter the room, hand each a pad of small Post-it™ notes and a pen or marker.

3. Ask participants to walk around the room individually or in small groups and consider the seven posters. They are to write responses to each poster question on a Post-it, and stick it on the poster. A person may respond with more than one idea, and everyone does not have to respond to every poster.

4. Give participants time to respond to at least a few of the posters, then call time.

5. Reposition all the posters up front so that everyone can see them. Review all (or some) of the responses with the whole group.

6. Ask participants to think about what it would take for them to make a similar valuable contribution to the local educational community.

7. Brainstorm ideas about how group members could support one another as teacher leaders.

8. Play Monte Selby's song "Who's Got That Vision?" If time is short, a scribe can take the posters and record all headings and responses for later distribution and discussion.

*(Optional Stopping Point—continue this session
or complete it in a follow-up session)*

9. Ask participants to turn to a partner and share why it is important for teachers to be leaders. Ask those partners to pair up with another set of partners and discuss what they decided.

10. Ask the groups of four to generate a list of obstacles that keep some teachers from becoming actively involved advancing within the profession. The lists should be written on poster paper.

11. Each group of four exchanges their poster with another group. After lists of obstacles are exchanged, the four-member groups should try to think of as many

Because You Teach

ideas as they can for overcoming the obstacles. They can write them on the posters or on a separate sheet of paper.

12. Ask for general feedback and suggestions for how administrators can help teachers become more effective advocates for students, the school, the district, and education in general.

Activities for a Small Group

Personal Teaching Visions

Purpose:

To challenge teachers to fulfill their personal visions for teaching

Materials:

- Copies of "My Vision for Myself" worksheet (page 121)
- Self-sealing envelopes

Step-by-step:

1. Review the large group session discussions about teacher greatness and teachers as leaders. Ask members to consider their personal teaching visions.

2. Hand out copies of the worksheet, along with self-sealing envelopes.

3. Have each teacher fill out the letter, seal it in the envelope, and write her/his name on the outside. Assure the participants that no one will see what they wrote, and you are going to put them in a secure place for the next few months.

4. Several months later, hand back the envelopes to their owners and ask them to reread their commitments to themselves. Ask them to reflect on whether or not they are any closer to their mission statements now than when they filled out the worksheet? Ask them to answer why or why not for themselves.

What Brought Me to This Point?

Purpose:

- To help participants pinpoint life events that have shaped them as teachers
- To give participants a chance to reflect on how their personal histories have influenced them as teachers and as teacher leaders

Materials:

- Notebook paper
- Pencils or pens
- Large sheet of art paper, butcher paper, or adding machine tape
- Marking pens

Step-by-step:

1. Ask participants to list on a sheet of paper the five worst and the five best things that have happened to them in their lives.

2. On the large paper or adding machine tape strips, have them create an individual timeline from their birth to the present, and plot the events they listed at their appropriate intervals. (They can use code words or initials on their timelines to maintain privacy, if they wish.)

3. On a separate sheet of paper, have them tell how each event prepared them for their roles as teachers and leaders in education.

4. In pairs or very small groups, ask participants to share their conclusions about what brought them to this place and time. (Group members can choose to skip any events they do not want to talk about.)

Guiding Questions:

   A. How did you feel at the time the event occurred?

   B. Did you have any idea about how influential the event would be to the rest of your life?

   C. How has the event shaped you as a teacher?

   D. How have you been able to capitalize on your experiences and use the lessons learned to become a better teacher and/or teacher leader?

Activities for Individuals

The Power of a Teacher Journal Activity

Purpose:

- To help teachers reflect on their individual power in the classroom
- To remind teachers of the influence they have on the future

Materials:

- Teacher journal or computer
- Pen or pencil or computer paper

Step-by-step:

1. Select a teacher who made a profound impact on your life.

2. List all the ways that the particular teachers made a difference in your life. Write about how your life might have been different had it not been for that teacher.

3. Pick three students (present or former) you believe have significantly influenced. Write about how you positively impacted those students' lives.

4. Select a difficult student you have currently in your class. Write a letter to yourself (the teacher) from the perspective of that student that you would like to receive in a few years. Think about what you could do now to make the chance of receiving a letter like that more likely.

5. Write an action plan for you to use with that student.

This Is What I Believe Journal Activity

Purpose:

- To help teachers reflect on their individual power in the classroom
- To remind teachers of the influence they have on the future

Materials:

- Teacher journal or computer
- Pen or pencil or computer paper

Step-by-step:

Select one of the quotations. Respond to it fully in your journal.

A. "I touch the future, I teach."

–Christa McAuliffe

B. "A teacher affects eternity; he can never tell where his influence stops . . ."

– Henry Brooks Adams

C. "What the teacher is, is more important than what he teaches."

– Karl Menninger

D. "Within every school there is a sleeping giant of teacher leadership, which can be a strong catalyst for making change. By using the energy of teacher leaders as agents of school change, the reform of public education will stand a better chance of building momentum."

– Marilyn Katzenmeyer and Gayle Moller, 2001.
Awakening the Sleeping Giant. Helping Teachers Develop as Leaders.
Thousand Oaks, CA, Corwin Press.

E. "Concerning a teacher's influence, I have come to the frightening conclusion that I am the decisive element in the classroom. It's my personal approach that creates the climate. It's my daily mood that makes the weather. As a teacher, I possess a tremendous power to make a child's life miserable or joyous. I can be a tool of torture or an instrument of inspiration. I can humiliate or humor, hurt or heal. In all situations, it is my response that decides whether a crisis will be escalated or de-escalated, and a child humanized or dehumanized."

– Haim Ginott

My Vision for Myself

Name _____

Date _____

Why I became a teacher: _____

_____

_____

_____

_____

_____

My most noble vision of myself as a teacher: _____

_____

_____

_____

_____

_____

What I am going to do over the next few months to reconcile my vision of myself at my greatest with my present circumstances:

_____

_____

_____

_____

_____

We're All in This Together

The Story Behind the Song

The idea for this song floated around in my head for a long time. I finally wrote it after September 11 with Blake Chaffin. I was Blake's elementary school music teacher and his middle school principal. When he went to college, I was completing my doctorate at the same college, and we played on the same intramural basketball team. Now Blake is a musician in Nashville. At each stage in our friendship, we really have been "in this together."

—Monte

Staff Development Ideas by Kathy Hunt-Ullock

The Focus

To help make teachers and staff feel that we are all indeed in this together and that each of us brings unique skills, personalities, expertise, and talents. When these talents are appreciated by all and are used to provide the best education possible for our students, there is no limit to what we can accomplish!

The Song

Athletic coaches, business leaders, medical professionals, and grade school relay teams recognize the importance of working together. They set goals, create a positive team image, recognize individual contributions, and commit to improving performance. Each productive team, regardless of its purpose, has members who share common goals and a common vision. Each member contributes to the team's success and is accountable for the end result. Members are dedicated to their personal goals, but are willing to act unselfishly. They recognize that whatever the size of the team,

Together

Everyone

Achieves

More

Is there a problem facing your staff or your school? Do you have new staff members that need to feel valued as important members of the learning team in your school? Are you looking for a way to pull your community and staff together? The lyrics of this song encourage educators (and community members) to join together to make the changes that need to be made. It's an upbeat way to salute the unity that is required for success.

The Hook

Recognize the participants that are part of your audience. Then simply say, "We're all in this together."

We're All in This Together

This is the time we begin to see things differently
To see things differently
It's not about me, it's not about you
Where we've been, what we've all been through
No this is about a brand new day
A new beginning, a better way.

CHORUS: We are all in this together
If we want to make a change
Every one of us committed
To give more than we take
Every age, every color
Hand in hand, as our neighbor
And we are all in this together.

So look around in your hometown,
You can help wherever you are
Yes, wherever you are
You don't have to be a hero;
Don't have to do it all.
Every little bit counts, no matter how small
When it all adds up, every role you play
Makes another strong link in a great big chain.

CHORUS: We are all in this together
If we want to make a change
Every one of us committed
Just to give more than we take
Every age, every color
Hand in hand, as our neighbor
And we are all in this together.

– Blake Chaffin and Monte Selby
©2002 Street Singer Music, BMI

Activity for a Large Group

The Human Number Line

Purpose:

To illustrate the idea that "no one is good at everything but everyone is good at something"

Materials:

- Ten pieces of poster board
- Marking pen

Step-by-step:

Prior to the activity, make a huge number line. Number the pieces of poster board. You will need a piece for each digit from 1 to 10. Make certain that the numbers are large and bold. Tape the numbers on a wall or lay them on the floor at least one foot apart so that group members can see all of the numbers.

1. Ask for six volunteers to be a part of the number line activity. When choosing the volunteers, make certain that you have included participants with a variety of ages, different sexes, different nationalities, different personalities, and different job responsibilities.

2. Have the chosen people stand near the number line.

3. Name a talent or skill. Here is a suggested list of talents to start you off:
   - a) singing
   - b) athletic ability
   - c) artistic ability
   - d) dancing
   - e) organizational skill
   - f) writing ability
   - g) love of the outdoors
   - h) public speaking ability
   - i) acting ability
   - j) musical instrument ability
   - k) juggling ability
   - l) curling of the tongue ability

If volunteers feel that they are REALLY good at that particular talent, they walk over and stand by the #10 on the number line. If they are REALLY terrible at this talent, they should stand by #1. Of course, they may also stand at any of the medial positions on the number line.

> ♪ Note: Make certain, once you see who is in the volunteer group, that you customize your categories so that you highlight a talent that you know someone does very well.

4. Once all of the people have moved and placed themselves on the number line, conduct a brief interview with each person. It works best when you interview the highest number person first. For example, if the talent you called off was "singing," ask this person when he first knew that he could sing, if he has ever sung professionally, etc. Next, go to the person who is standing by the lowest number and interview him or her. End with interviewing the people individually in the center spots.

5. Once all the folks on the number line have had a chance to respond, call out a different talent and watch the line move. Repeat the interview process by mixing up who is interviewed first. Call out as many talents as time allows.

6. After you are done, thank the volunteers and reiterate that no one is good at everything, but everyone is good at something. It takes ALL of us working together to make the best education possible for our kids! Also, remind teachers that the same goes for the students that we teach. They all have different talents and abilities, and it is our job to find them and teach to them, not against them!

Follow-up Activity:

Have each grade level, team, department, advisory, or seminar group do this same activity with students and report back at the next faculty meeting.

Activities for a Small Group

Playing to Each Other's Strengths

Purpose:

To encourage team members to share strengths and weaknesses

Materials:

- 4" x 6" index cards
- Pencils

Step-by-step:

1. During the next two weeks, visit a grade level, team, or department meeting. Hand out a 4" x 6" index card to each person.

2. Have group members write a plus sign in the upper-left corner of one side of the card and a minus sign in the upper-left corner of the reverse side.

3. Give participants five minutes to fill out the card.

    - On the plus side, ask them to make a list of all the positive qualities, knowledge, and expertise that they bring to this organization. For example, a person may list such things as a sense of humor, a deep knowledge of multiple intelligences, a good hands-on instructor, an in-depth knowledge of the district science curriculum, etc.

    - Then, on the reverse side, ask them to list those things that bug them and the things that they are still working on to improve. For example, a person may list such things as an intolerance of people who are consistently late, still working on improving their computer skills, not a very good writer, etc.

4. After the time is up, go around the room and ask the participants to share both sides of the card with their peers. If we truly are "all in this together," it is important that we understand the strengths and weaknesses of ourselves and our colleagues. That knowledge can help us better delegate tasks and work more closely as a highly functioning team of professionals. Once again, we will discover that no one is good at everything but everyone is good at something!

Pipe Cleaner Sculptures

Purpose:

To emphasize the importance of working together

Materials:

Colored pipe cleaners (5 per person)

Step-by-step:

1. Place participants in heterogeneous groups of four to six members. Give each group a number.

2. Hand out five different-colored pipe cleaners to each person.

3. Ask participants to create a pipe cleaner sculpture using only the five pipe cleaners that they received. The sculpture should reveal something about themselves . For example, a person may create a pine tree with the sun above because they love the mountains and the outdoors. Another person may create a heart with a dog attached, as they just purchased a new puppy and it is the little love of their life. Allow about ten minutes for the folks to create their sculptures.

4. After the sculptures are completed, ask participants to share their sculptures within the group.

5. Have the group create ONE BIG sculpture by combining all of their little sculptures and labeling the name of their group at the top of their new BIG creation. For example, if this is group Team 7-A, they MAY use additional pipe cleaners to construct a "7-A" on top of the sculpture, and then hang all of the little sculptures from the newly constructed 7-A.

   > ♪ Note: There are no rules here. It is the labeling that is important.

   OR, if this is the MATH department, the group may wish to make the word MATH from the new pipe cleaners, and hang all of the little sculptures from the word MATH.

6. An administrator may collect the sculptures from all teams in the school. A cart with wheels will be a big help! Once all of the group sculptures have been collected, it is the administrator's job (with any help he chooses to solicit) to create a huge sculpture that places all of the group sculptures into one.

7. Present this new creation at the next faculty meeting—a symbol that "we are all in this together." Attach it to the ceiling of the teachers' lounge as a symbol of unity.

> ♪ Note: Teachers could do a similar activity with their students through advisory or homeroom. Each student creates and shares a little sculpture. Then, each advisory or homeroom creates a larger sculpture and labels that sculpture. This new creation could be attached to the ceiling of their classroom. If you wish to go further, you could then create larger and larger sculptures, depending on the organizational structure of the school, to eventually create a HUGE school-wide structure and place it on the ceiling of a common student area. Of course, be cognizant of code and fire violations!

Together We're Better

Purpose:

To visually illustrate how educators are interconnected

Materials:

- Newsprint or poster board
- Marking pens or crayons

Step-by-step:

1. Place participants in heterogeneous groups of four to six. Give each group a number.

2. Give each table a sheet of newsprint or poster board and a variety of colored marking pens or crayons.

3. Have each group make a diagram illustrating how "we're all in this together" and ways that we are all connected in the school. There are no rules.

4. Give participants 10 to 15 minutes to create their diagrams, and tell them that when their group number is called, they must share the diagram and explain it to the entire group.

5. Randomly call out table numbers and have as many groups share their diagrams as time allows.

Activity for Individuals

The Good and the Bad of Togetherness

Purpose:

To allow individuals time to reflect on the positive impact of interdependence as well as its drawbacks

Materials:

- Journal or computer
- Pen and pencil or computer paper

Step-by-step:

1. Think about positive ways that working together can affect the students in your classroom. Record your ideas.

2. Think about negative ways that working together can affect the students in your classroom. After recording the ideas, think of safeguards you might implement to ensure that the negative influences are minimized.

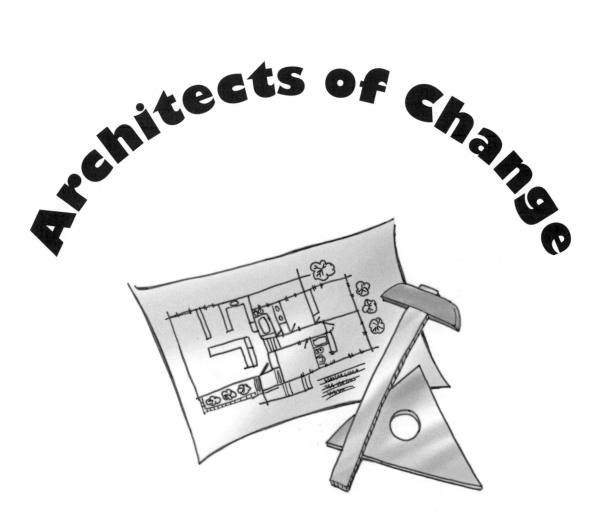

Architects of Change

The Story Behind the Song

"Architects of Change" was the theme for the 2004 NASSP National Convention. Prior to the convention, I worked with the steering committee to write a song that would encourage principals to attend the meeting. I also performed the song at the convention, where I was surprised to find that it was a favorite with educators. If you like exploring leadership, this could be your song!

—Monte

Staff Development Ideas by Kathy Hunt-Ullock

The Focus

To help empower teachers to take risks, both personally and professionally, in providing the best educational experience for their students and colleagues.

The Song

How often do we as leaders in the field of education take time to consider the value of sharing our problems and solutions, to consider change, and to celebrate our common purpose? *Architects of Change* gives us that opportunity.

The Hook

To set the stage for this activity, read the following "one-liners" about change to the entire group:

a) As long as you don't change anything, I'm flexible.

b) It is easier to ride a horse in the direction that it's facing.

c) Leading and managing change in schools is like changing a tire while the car is moving.

d) It is easy to go downstream. Even a dead fish can do that.

e) Change always involves risk. You can't keep one foot on first base and steal second.

f) People seem to be more resistant to the process of change than they are to the change itself.

g) Past experience should be a guidepost, not a hitching post.

h) Remember, change is a process, not an event.

i) To grow is to change, and to become perfect is to change many times.

j) We're not where we should be, we're not where we're going to be, but thank goodness we're not where we used to be!

k) You don't have to be sick to get better!

l) When the horse dies, dismount!

Now, tell the audience to relax, sit back, listen to the song "Architects of Change," and think globally about the power of working together to bring about change in their school.

Because You Teach

Architects of Change

For all the right reasons come take a little time
Share your commitment with thousands who find
That together we learn, we support, and we dream
We design and we plan and more children succeed.

CHORUS: In our hands, there is power to create.
          In our hearts, a mission to embrace.
          We can look down the road to a future,
          Draw a blueprint that guides us today.
          Join the vision of leaders becoming
                         the Architects of Change.

For all the right reasons bring colleagues and friends
Overwhelmed by the worries, the issues, the trends.
We're all looking for answers for our cities and towns
To lay strong foundations let's start building now.

CHORUS: In our hands, there is power to create.
          In our hearts, a mission to embrace.
          We can look down the road to a future,
          Draw a blueprint that guides us today.
          Join the vision of leaders becoming
                         the Architects of Change.

– Monte Selby
©2004 Street Singer Music, BMI

Activities for a Large Group

The One Thing

Purpose:

To reflect on the past school year and to work in groups to come to an agreement on THE ONE THING to change for the following school year

Materials:

- Index cards
- Writing tools
- Poster boards
- Red stickers

Step-by-step:

1. Read the following statement by Peter Drucker: *"The best way to predict the future is to create it!"* Then tell the group that they are now going to help "create" their next school year.

2. Ask each person to take their large index card and write down an idea that they would change for the next school year. It could be a BIG "thing" like an adjustment to the master schedule, or a smaller "thing" like offering a certain food in the cafeteria. Give them about three minutes to do this.

3. Now, have each person share their idea with the other people at their table.

4. After sharing, the group must agree on the ONE idea that they feel is the most important "thing" to change for the following school year. One idea is allowed per table.

5. Each table now is called upon to share their table's idea for change with the whole group.

6. Each table's "winning" card is then collected, and a whole group list of ideas is compiled by the office.

Follow-up Activities

- Sometime during the next two weeks, a member(s) of the administration will visit grade level, team, or department meetings to discuss the compiled list and make priorities for change based on the discussions.

- The administration could list each table's winning idea on a piece of poster board and hang the posters on the wall of the teachers' lounge. People would then be asked to write comments on the poster boards about that particular idea. After a period of time, the comments on the poster boards would be compiled. Finally, as suggested in activity above, a member(s) of the administration would visit grade level, team, or department meetings to discuss the comments and make priorities.

Communication Cards

Purpose:

By communicating with picture cards, groups will share five things that they like about their school and three things that they would change.

Materials (for each group):

- Packs of picture cards reproduced from the patterns on pages 142 and 143
- Paper and pencils

Step-by-step:

1. Place people in heterogeneous groups of 4 to 6.

2. Give each group one set of picture cards consisting of 24 different pictures.

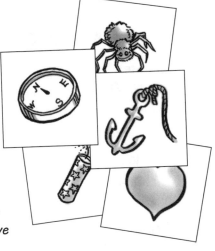

3. Ask one person in each group to remove the rubber band from the cards and spread out all 24 cards on the table FACEUP so that everyone in the group can see all of the pictures.

4. The group now has five minutes to choose five cards that represent five things that they like about their school. Each person in the group must agree on all five cards. The facilitator for this activity should inform the groups when there is one minute left to go.

5. Next, each group must pick a spokesperson who, when their table number is called, will stand, show each of the five cards their group chose, and explain why they picked each card.

6. Call upon as many tables as time allows.

7. Next, have each group choose three pictures that represent three things that they would change about their school. Once again, give the groups five minutes to do this .

> ♪ Note: Have fun with the following method of picking a spokesperson:
> Tell each person to choose a spokesperson for their group in their mind only. Don't let anyone in their group know who they are choosing. Once each person has chosen a person in their mind, tell them to place both hands flat on the table in front of them. At the count of three, they will pound their hands on the table three times and then POINT to the person in their group that they have chosen to be the group spokesperson. Only one finger per person counts. The person with the most fingers pointing at them gets the job! If there is a tie, and this will frequently occur, ask the people that the tie is between to write down their home phone number on a piece of scrap paper. The person with the highest last digit gets the job. If there is still a tie, go to the second to the last digit, etc., until the tie is broken.

8. Call on a few tables that were not called upon during the first round to share the three things that they would change.

9. Ask each spokesperson to write down the three things that their group would change and submit the list to the office by the end of the day.

Activities for a Small Group

The Story of the Lobster

Purpose:

- To listen to a story about personal and professional growth
- To make plans to do something different
- To recognize peers for their accomplishment(s) in this area

Materials:

- Copies of the lobster coupon (page 141)
- (optional) Plastic lobsters

Step-by-step:

1. Read the following story aloud to the group:

Once there was a little boy who was visiting an aquarium. He was gazing into the lobster tank with a very curious look on his face. An aquarium attendant noticed that the little boy was spending a great deal of time looking at the lobsters, so he wandered over and asked the boy if he had any questions. The little boy asked, "I can see that there are many different sizes of lobsters in the tank, and I know that their shells are very hard. Just how does a lobster grow bigger with those hard shells?"

The attendant smiled and told the boy that the only way for a lobster to grow was to shed its shell at regular intervals. When its body begins to feel cramped inside the shell, the lobster instinctively looks for a safe place to rest while the hard shell comes off and the pink membrane just inside forms the basis of the next shell. This process takes about 72 hours. But no matter where a lobster goes for the shedding process, it is very vulnerable. It can get tossed against a coral reef or eaten by a fish. In other words, a lobster literally risks its life in order to grow.

The little boy was fascinated by this information, and after gazing into the tank for a few more minutes, thanked the attendant and went on his merry way.

In many ways, all of us are like lobsters. We all really know when our shells have gotten too tight. We can feel angry or depressed or frightened because life is no longer exciting or challenging. We keep doing the same old things and may be beginning to feel bored, or we are doing things that we hate and are feeling stifled in our shells. Some of us continue to smother in old shells that are no longer useful or productive. That way, we can at least feel safe—nothing can happen to us. Others are luckier; even though we know that we will be vulnerable, that there are dangers ahead, we realize that we must take risks or suffocate.

2. After reading this story aloud to the audience, hand out the "Lobster Coupon" to each person OR buy little plastic lobsters at a discount store and give one to each person. If plastic lobsters are purchased, ask the teachers to place them on their desks in their classrooms as a constant reminder that they are working in a "safe place" where risk is valued and encouraged. If the lobster coupon is used, ask teachers to place them in their wallets and carry them around with them. Extra copies of the coupons should be made and placed in the office. When a person sees another person taking a risk and trying something new, they should be encouraged to give that person a lobster coupon with a congratulatory note attached. You could go nuts with this lobster stuff!

3. Tell the audience that you want them to try new things, to risk, and to grow but in order to do that, you are going to create a "safe place" for them to be successful. The lobster picture or toy will remind everyone that they are working in a safe, creative environment, and that periodically they can "shed their shells."

4. End this activity by reading the following to the audience:

   a) Change happens best when people:
- feel comfortable
- feel gratified
- feel in control
- feel safe
- feel confident

   b) "A ship in port is safe, but that's not what ships are built for."

Follow-up Activities:

- Sometime during the next two weeks, the principal would visit a grade level, team, or department meeting and ask the group how they could best help create that safe environment where each group would feel "safe" enough to take a few risks and grow both personally and professionally. Once those ideas are shared, the principal would then ask the group to commit to three new things that they will try during the new school year. For example, a team might commit to keeping a weekly log of activities they are doing with kids coded to each of the Multiple Intelligences described by Howard Gardner, or they may commit to looking at new ways to recognize kids for their accomplishments.

- Begin a "LOBSTER(s) OF THE MONTH" program for teachers. At a faculty meeting, one or more teachers will be saluted for trying something new. To make this enjoyable, one could purchase rubber lobster claws, head pieces, or big rubber lobsters and award them to folks along with a big lobster coupon and a free dinner to a Red Lobster restaurant!

Activity for Individuals

Just a Note

Purpose:

- To commit to a plan for personal growth
- To acknowledge perceived changes

Materials:

- Notepaper
- Pens

Step-by-Step

1. Compose a note to the principal. The note should list THREE new things that you will do differently during the new school year.

2. The principal will compile the notes, without names, and share the compiled list with the entire faculty so that people can see the changes being made and the risks being taken.

Lobster Coupons

You are in a safe place.

It's okay to try something new.

You are in a safe place.

It's okay to try something new.

You are in a safe place.

It's okay to try something new.

Cards

Because You Teach
©2006 by Incentive Publications, Inc./Street Singer Books, Nashville, TN

Cards